# TENNYSON
## 1809-1892

Cat. 21 Tennyson by Julia Margaret Cameron - 'The Dirty Monk'

# TENNYSON
## 1809-1892

## A CENTENARY CELEBRATION

ROBERT WOOF

THE WORDSWORTH TRUST
1992

ISBN 0 90195 830 1

# Contents

# Lenders to the Exhibition

Her Majesty The Queen

Aberdeen Art Gallery
Birmingham City Art Gallery
Bristol University
British Museum, London
Edmund Brudenell Esq., Deene Park Collection, Corby, Northants
Campbell Fine Art, London
Mr Roy Davids Collection
Mr Oliver Davies Collection
Lady Elton
Eton College
Eton School
The Syndics of The Fitzwilliam Museum
The Garrick Club, London
Keith Hanley Collection
Lord Henley Collection
County Archives, Lincolnshire County Council
Jeremy Maas Galleries, London
Miles Mallinson, Barrow-in-Furness, Cumbria
George Mandl Collection
Matheison Art Gallery, London
Mr Michael Meredith Collection
Dorothy Milnes Collection
Mr John Moxon Collection
National Museum of Photography, Film and Television, Bradford
National Museum of Wales, Cardiff
Mr Peter Nahum, 5 Ryder Street, London
National Portrait Gallery, London
Penrith Museum
Ruth Pitman Collection
Pre-Raphaelite Inc., by courtesy of Julian Hartnoll
17th/21st Lancers Regimental Museum, Prince William Gloucester Barracks, Grantham, Lincs
The Royal Society, London
Southampton City Art Gallery
Spedding Collection
The Earl of Stockton and the Macmillan Family Trustees
The Trustees of The Tate Gallery, London
Tennyson Research Centre, Linconshire County Council
Tennyson Society
The Fellows of Trinity College, Cambridge
Tullie House, Carlisle
Victoria and Albert Museum, London
The Watts Gallery, Guildford
Whitworth Art Gallery, Manchester
Stephen Wildman Collection
Wolverhampton Art Gallery
The Wordsworth Trust, Dove Cottage, Grasmere

Among the generous owners who have lent to the Exhibition several wish to remain anonymous.

# Acknowledgments

The Trustees of The Wordsworth Trust would like to thank the many people and institutions who have helped make this exhibition to celebrate the life and work of Tennyson. Tennyson died one hundred years ago, in October 1892. The Exhibition opened in Grasmere, 1 March 1992 (closes 23 June), and continues, with many additional items, at the Usher Gallery, Lincoln, 7 July - 12 September 1992.

We would like to thank first, Kathleen Jefferson, whose diplomacy and imagination opened the way for The Wordsworth Trust, The Tennyson Society and Lincolnshire County Council to bring their resources together for this joint enterprise. Second, Sue Gates who at The Tennyson Research Centre gave us all necessary support in sorting through the great hoard and wealth of that collection. Third, David McKitterick from Trinity College, Cambridge (along with his Deputy, Ronald Milne) who facilitated our research into their major collection of Tennyson's manuscripts. We have much appreciated Richard Wood's contribution to our planning in his role as curator at The Usher Gallery. Many other institutions who have lent their treasures are listed separately and are warmly thanked. Some individuals have been particularly helpful: David Scrase of The Fitzwilliam Museum, Cambridge; Stephen Wildman of Birmingham City Art Gallery; Francina Irwin of Aberdeen City Art Gallery; Reg Alton; Julian Cox of the National Museum of Photography, Film and Television; Mrs Sheila Edwards of the Royal Society; Julian Hartnoll; Jeremy Maas; Joanna Barnes; Ruth Pitman; and John and Claire Spedding. Lady Elton's kindness in allowing so much of the Hallam material to be lent, added to the scholarship of Paul Quarrie of Eton College Library, has made Hallam a central figure in the exhibition.

We are greatly indebted to Her Majesty the Queen for the loans of the Fenton material, the drawings by the Royal Princesses, and the presentation copies given by Tennyson to Queen Victoria. We are grateful not only for the generosity and the loans, but for the kind research support and the overall help we have had: an incomplete list must include Lady de Bellaigue, Oliver Everett, Teresa Mary-Morton, Frances Dimond, Bridget Wright and David Westwood. They have helped make the the arrangements for creating this exhibition such a pleasurable experience. Many more should be thanked, but I should be embarrassed not to mention the following: Geoffrey Blake, Michael Campbell, Susan Lambert, Lionel Lambourne, Rupert Maas, Michael Meredith, Roger Taylor, Derek Wise.

We are particularly thankful to Sotheby's for their great kindness in helping with the preparation of the Catalogue - to Amanda Brooks (who did not panic), and to Roy Davids for his affirmative and always encouraging voice. Through Oliver Turnbull, our printer (and daily support), we have come to appreciate new delicacies in the Art of the Possible. The Catalogue has benefitted from financial support from the Tennyson Society, Trinity College, Cambridge, and John Spedding.

Among our staff at Grasmere there have been countless gestures of good will and kindness. I thank Michael McGregor for helping over two years in the choice of exhibits, Jeff Cowton for his meticulous work as Registrar and his no less fine work as designer, Joanne Gunnion and David Green for their exemplary dedication, Alex Black for his zest in the photography, and Stephen Hebron for his careful research, his drafting and composing many of the notes, and his finesse in bringing together the typescript of the Catalogue. Notes on the poems have benefitted from the insights of Pamela Woof.

We are grateful to British Gas for their support of the Education Programme.

Robert Woof
Director, The Wordsworth Trust
June 1992

# A Tennyson Chronology

## 1809

**6 August:** Alfred Tennyson was born in Lincolnshire, at Somersby Rectory, the fourth (and third surviving) child of the Rev George Clayton Tennyson, Rector of Somersby and his wife Elizabeth Fytche. His father was the elder son of George Tennyson of Bayons Manor, Tealby, who had disinherited George Clayton in favour of his younger son Charles (later Charles Tennyson D'Eyncourt). This decision caused great bitterness between the two branches of the family, casting a shadow over much of Tennyson's early life. In the eleven years following his birth eight more children were born, making a total of seven boys and four girls.

## 1813

The Tennyson family went on holiday to Mablethorpe on the Lincolnshire coast. Tennyson used the coast as the basis for many descriptions of the sea.

## 1816

**December:** Tennyson was sent to join his elder brothers, Frederick and Charles, at Louth Grammar School, where he remained for three years; unlike them he was a day-boy, living with his grandmother, Mrs Fytche, and his aunt, Mary Ann Fytche. The school was marred by sadistic schoolmasters and bullying boys, and hated by Tennyson.

## 1818

George Tennyson, Tennyson's grandfather, and Charles Tennyson, his uncle, were both returned as Members of Parliament in the General Election.

## 1820

Tennyson was removed from Louth Grammar School to be taught, as in his early years, by his father, a highly educated man but an erratic tutor. George Clayton Tennyson suffered from epilepsy and this, combined with heavy drinking, led to moods of black depression and violent rages. Tennyson, not without some encouragement from his father, took these occasions to write verse himself and to read widely in the poetry of others.

## 1823

About this time, Tennyson wrote *The Devil and the Lady,* a three-act comedy in blank verse, his style echoing *Hamlet, King Lear* and *The Tempest,* as well as *Paradise Lost.*

## 1823

With George Clayton Tennyson's behaviour becoming increasingly violent and unpredictable, Tennyson gradually assumed responsibility for the household.

## 1827

**April:** Jacksons, the booksellers at Louth, produced *Poems by. Two Brothers,* Tennyson's first appearance in print. He had written more than half the poems; most of the others were by his brother Charles, whilst a few were by his eldest brother Frederick.

**June:** Tennyson and Charles visit George Clayton Tennyson's wealthy and recently widowed sister, Elizabeth Russell - probably the first time they had left Lincolnshire.

**9 November:** Tennyson, helped financially by Aunt Russell, entered Trinity College, Cambridge. Charles and Frederick were already at Cambridge. The three brothers stood out from other students, in appearance, unconventional behaviour, and in their intellectual and literary promise.

## 1828

**October:** Arthur Henry Hallam entered Trinity as a student.

## 1829

**Spring:** Tennyson met Arthur Hallam for the first time. Hallam quickly became Tennyson's closest friend and had a profound influence on his life. Intellectually gifted, he was obviously a man of great charm, highly regarded by many of his contemporaries.

**6 June:** Tennyson was awarded The Chancellor's Gold Medal for his poem 'Timbuctoo'. His friend Charles Merivale read the poem at the Senate House, Tennyson blaming shyness for his failure to read the poem for himself.

**Summer:** Tennyson returned to a quiet Somersby, his father being away in France. During the summer the family held several parties and it was probably at one of these that Tennyson first met his future wife, Emily Sellwood. Emily was one of three daughters of Henry Sellwood, a Horncastle solicitor. Their uncle was the explorer Sir John Franklin. In 1829 she was sixteen, a similar age to Tennyson's sisters, her friends Emily and Mary.

**31 October:** Tennyson was elected to the brilliant if secretive Cambridge Conversazione Society, usually referred to ironically as 'The Cambridge Apostles', ('Apostles' being slang for those who were the bottom twelve in the final examinations). Although he was a member for only a very short time, his name remains associated with the group because of the friendships it gave him. Formed in 1820, the Society was enlivened four years later by F.D. Maurice, Tennyson's future friend, and John Sterling. In discussions its members gave papers on politics, science, poetry and related subjects.

**December:** Arthur Hallam visited Somersby for the first time and there met Alfred's younger sister, Emily, to whom he later became engaged.

## 1830

**13 February:** Tennyson resigned his membership of the Apostles, apparently too uneasy to give a paper or to speak in the discussions. He had attended only five meetings, but the friendships remained.

**June:** *Poems, Chiefly Lyrical* was published. Tennyson had earlier hoped to publish in conjunction with Arthur Hallam but, following objections from Hallam's father, had finally gone ahead alone.

**July:** Tennyson and Arthur Hallam go to the Pyrenees. Their purpose was ostensibly to take money and dispatches to the Spanish revolutionaries who were assembling there. Their interest had been aroused through the Cambridge Apostles, and they became acquainted with various Spanish exiles, especially with the charismatic Torrijos, who had fled to England following the restoration of King Ferdinand to the Spanish throne in 1823. The revolutionaries aimed to regain power in Spain, but when Tennyson and Hallam met with their representative and

discovered their murderous, anti-clerical zeal, a disillusionment set in. However, the journey to the valley of Cauteretz in the Pyrenees had a profound effect on Tennyson and he returned more than once to the area, many of his memories being reflected in the imagery of his poetry.

## 1831

**February:** Tennyson and Charles left Cambridge without taking their degrees in order to be at the bedside of their father, now in declining health.

**16 March:** George Clayton Tennyson died. Tennyson's grandfather provided quite generously for the Somersby family, but the bitterness remained, and the plea of poverty was one which all the Tennysons were to use throughout their lives.

**August:** Arthur Hallam reviewed *Poems, Chiefly Lyrical* in *The Englishman's Magazine*, a journal published by Edward Moxon. Hallam introduced Tennyson's poetry to Moxon, who agreed to publish future volumes. This marked the beginning of Tennyson's long association with his first regular publisher.

## 1832

**May:** An unfavourable review of *Poems, Chiefly Lyrical* by John Wilson, 'Christopher North', appeared in *Blackwood's Magazine*. Tennyson reacted strongly to the criticism and throughout his life remained sensitive to any adverse reviews of his work.

**July:** Tennyson visited the Rhineland with Arthur Hallam.

**December:** *Poems* 1833 was published by Moxon during the first week of December. Nearly a hundred copies were sold during the first two days. However, the reviews were generally unfavourable, particularly one by Edward Bulwer-Lytton in *The New Monthly Magazine* of January 1833.

## 1833

**April:** Arthur Hallam's engagement to Emily Tennyson, to whom he had been writing affectionately for three years, was finally recognised by his father, Henry Hallam.

**Summer:** Tennyson's uncle Charles Tennyson

moved into Bayons Manor, Tealby, and began the process of changing the family name to Tennyson D'Eyncourt.

**15 September:** Arthur Hallam died from apoplexy whilst in Vienna with his father. The Tennysons were the first people outside the family to be notified of his death; the news was sent to Tennyson in a letter from Hallam's uncle, Henry Elton, at the beginning of October.

### 1834

**6 October:** Tennyson began the first of his elegies dedicated to Arthur Hallam, lyrics which some thirteen years later were to become a part of *In Memoriam*.

**23 September:** Alfred wrote a poem for the birthday of Rosa Baring with whom he was said to be infatuated. She had been friendly with the Tennyson family since the autumn of 1832 soon after she came to live at Harrington Hall, near Somersby, with her stepfather Arthur Eden. Her friendship with Tennyson developed at parties and family gatherings. From 1834-36 Tennyson wrote a dozen poems either directly or indirectly about Rosa. By 1836 the romance had cooled and in 1838 she married Robert Shafto.

### 1835

**March:** Tennyson's brother Charles Tennyson inherited the estate of his great uncle Samuel Turner and added the name of Turner to his own to comply with the terms of the will.

**April:** Tennyson visited James Spedding, a Cambridge friend second only to Hallam, at Mirehouse, the home of Spedding's family on the shores of Bassenthwaite, near Keswick, in the Lake District. Another guest was a schoolfriend of Spedding's, Edward Fitzgerald, whom Tennyson had also briefly met at Cambridge. He was the eccentric son of a rich family and is largely remembered for his version of *The Rubaiyat of Omar Khayyam*, first published in 1859. This meeting with Tennyson led to a lifelong friendship. After Fitzgerald left, Tennyson and Spedding visited Wordsworth at Rydal Mount.

**4 July:** George Tennyson, Alfred's grandfather died. Under the terms of his will the family were left comfortably provided for

but the Somersby family bitterly compared their fortunes with the inheritance of their uncle, Charles.

**31 July:** Charles Tennyson was granted a royal licence to allow him to add D'Eyncourt to his name. He then began transforming Bayons Manor from a modest manor house into a Gothic fairy-tale castle complete with moat.

**September:** Charles Tennyson Turner became engaged to Louisa Sellwood, younger sister of Emily Sellwood.

### 1836

**24 May:** Charles Tennyson Turner married Louisa Sellwood. At the wedding, Tennyson, as groomsman, was paired with the bridesmaid Emily Sellwood. Within a short time of the wedding they became unofficially engaged.

### 1837

**Spring:** The family moved to Beech Hill House in Epping Forest, to make way for the new Rector of Somersby. Tennyson never again lived in Lincolnshire, although, at first, he did make frequent visits to friends, often staying with the Sellwoods. His life becomes solitary and nomadic for the next thirteen years.

### 1839

Tennyson's engagement to Emily Sellwood was broken off for reasons never fully explained. He became increasingly pre-occupied with his lack of money, although by most contemporary standards he was never poor.

### 1840

**Summer:** All contact between Tennyson and Emily Sellwood was severed and over the next decade there is little evidence of any communication between them. Emily Sellwood continued to live with her father, eventually moving with him from Lincolnshire to Hampshire.

The Tennyson family moved from High Beech to 5 Grove Hill, Tunbridge Wells, a house and town which Tennyson hated.

During the summer Tennyson returned to High Beech to visit his brother Septimus, who was a voluntary patient at the enlightened asylum for the insane run by Matthew Allen. Dr. Allen was a pioneer of the 'voluntary patient' system, and he and Tennyson soon became friends.

**23 November:** Tennyson and other members of the family invest heavily in Matthew Allen's money-making scheme of wood-carvings made on steam driven machines. By the end of 1842 the scheme was in ruins and the Tennysons lost almost all they invested.

## 1841

**March:** Tennyson met Robert Browning for the first time.

At the end of 1841 the family moved from Tunbridge Wells to Boxley Hall, near Maidstone.

## 1842

**14 May:** Despite Tennyson's anxiety over the wood-carving scheme, he continued writing, and published *Poems 1842* which eventually became the best loved of his volumes of miscellaneous poems. The first volume contained poems taken from *Poems, Chiefly Lyrical* and *Poems 1833*, including the revised 'Oenone', 'The Lady of Shalott', 'The Palace of Art' and 'The Lotos-Eaters', in the form that they are now known to modern readers. The second volume included 'Ulysses', 'Morte D'Arthur', 'St Simeon Stylites', 'Locksley Hall' and 'Break, Break, Break', to name but some. The reviews were generally favourable and established Tennyson as the outstanding poet of his generation.

## 1843

**March:** Robert Southey, the Poet Laureate died. At first it was thought that Tennyson might be appointed but eventually the honour went to William Wordsworth.

**November/December:** The family again moved, from Boxley Hall (which had proved too expensive) to Bellevue Place, Cheltenham.

## 1844

By the end of the year Tennyson's health had so deteriorated that he decided to admit himself for a 'water cure' and during the rest of the 1840s Tennyson visited at least three

establishments for similar treatment. His fear was that he had inherited his father's epilepsy and depressive temperament.

## 1845

Although, during his illnesses, Tennyson had written little except further elegies for *In Memoriam* his reputation as a poet continued to grow. He was granted a Civil List pension after the intervention of some influential friends, including Gladstone and the poet Samuel Rogers.

## 1847

**25 December:** *The Princess* was published, the first edition selling out within a couple of months. By 1851 there had been four editions. The reviews were mixed, with some of the critics feeling that Tennyson had not yet reached his full potential.

## 1848

**May-July:** Tennyson visited Cornwall, toying with the idea of a work on Arthurian themes, already touched on in his brilliant 'Morte D'Arthur'.

**July:** Tennyson became a patient at Dr. Gully's water establishment in Malvern, where he had stayed on a previous occasion. Gully informed him that he was suffering from gout not epilepsy and this marked the end of Tennyson's 'water cures'.

By the end of 1848 Tennyson's finances were so much improved that Moxon was able to convince him that he could make a living from his poetry.

## 1849

**January:** Edward Moxon saw the manuscript of *In Memoriam*, which he urged Tennyson to publish. Tennyson would not commit himself.

**24 November:** Tennyson sent to Emily Sellwood two versions of his poem 'Sweet and Low' for the new edition of *The Princess*, asking her to choose between them, thus renewing their acquaintance.

## 1850

**Mid-March:** Moxon printed the first trial run of *In Memoriam*. Copies were sent to Tennyson's closest friends for comment.

**1 June:** The first edition of *In Memoriam* was published anonymously. The poem, dedicated to the memory of Arthur Hallam, was an instant success, finding favour with almost all the critics, and reached its fourth edition within a few months of publication. *In Memoriam* transformed Tennyson's life, establishing him as the foremost poet of the age and ensuring him financial security.

**13 June:** Tennyson and Emily Sellwood were married at Shiplake, fourteen years after they had become unofficially engaged. Emily's cousin and Tennyson's friend Drummond Rawnsley performed the ceremony. The honeymoon began with a visit to Hallam's grave at Clevedon; it continued with a stay in the Lakes, first with the Speddings at Mirehouse and then at Tent Lodge, a house on the shores of Coniston.

**5 November:** Tennyson accepted the appointment of Poet Laureate, vacant since the death of Wordsworth on 23 April. For the Queen and Prince Albert, Tennyson was the preferred choice.

## 1851

**26 February:** Tennyson went to London for a levée where he was presented to the Queen as Poet Laureate, wearing the 'court dress' (a formal velvet suit) formerly lent to Wordsworth for a similar occasion by Samuel Rogers.

**Spring:** Alfred and Emily Tennyson moved to Chapel House, Twickenham. They had lived very briefly at 'The Hill' in Warninglid near Horsham but the house was so uncomfortable that they decided to move after one night in the place.

**April:** Emily gave birth to a stillborn baby boy.

## 1852

**11 August:** Hallam Tennyson was born. The Tennysons wanted to move from Twickenham and after the birth of Hallam their search for a new home intensified.

## 1853

**11 November:** Tennyson signed a three year lease for Farringford, the house which became the family home on the Isle of Wight. By the end of the month the family were in residence. From this time Emily, despite her frail health, played a very important role in organising Tennyson's life. She acted as his secretary, dealing with most of the correspondence, managed the efficient running of the household, kept up a stream of visitors to entertain Tennyson and, at the same time, ensured that he had the solitude he needed for his writing.

## 1854

**16 March:** Lionel Tennyson was born.

**2 December:** Tennyson wrote one of his best known poems, 'The Charge of the Light Brigade', after reading the account of the Battle of Balaclava in *The Times*.

**9 December:** ' The Charge of the Light Brigade' was published in *The Examiner*. The poem proved so popular that within a few months Tennyson had 1,000 copies privately printed to send to the troops at Sevastopol.

## 1855

**June:** Tennyson received an honorary doctorate from Oxford University.

## 1855

**28 July:** *Maud and other poems* was published. Much to Tennyson's surprise the poem was severely criticised, probably because it was so different from his last major work, *In Memoriam*. Despite the criticism, however, the poem sold 8,000 copies within two months of publication. Tennyson himself took every opportunity to read *Maud* aloud to his friends.

**31 December:** Tennyson attended a literary gathering given by Lady Ashburton. As Tennyson's reputation grew so did his circle of friends and he was now mixing freely with the aristocracy.

## 1856

**Early May:** Prince Albert visited Farringford.

**May:** The Tennysons buy Farringford.

## 1857

Moxon published an illustrated edition of Tennyson's poems, commissioning some of the finest artists of the age.

## 1858

**2 June:** Edward Moxon, Tennyson's publisher, died. Although relations between the two had not always been good, it is generally felt that Moxon understood Tennyson's working methods better than any of his other publishers. With diminishing success, Moxon's widow, with her sons yet minors, tried to continue her husband's work through a manager. Over the next few years Tennyson turned to a number of publishers, including Henry S. King, Alexander Strahan, and Routledge, Kegan Paul.

## 1859

**June:** The first book to bear the title *Idylls of the King* (containing *Enid, Vivien, Elaine and Guinevere*), was published. Tennyson had long been interested in the Arthurian legends and this publication marked the beginning of a series of works on the *Idylls*, which increased from four verse tales to ten. Of the 40,000 copies printed more than 10,000 had been sold within a few weeks of publication.

## 1860

Julia Margaret Cameron, the brilliant, if eccentric, Victorian photographer moved to Freshwater, Isle of Wight, as a neighbour of the Tennysons. During her fifteen years on the island, Mrs Cameron became an integral part of its lively artistic environment and an intimate of Tennyson.

**Summer:** Tennyson travels to Devon and Cornwall. Over the years many of Tennyson's old-established travelling companions had been replaced by younger men such as the writers Francis Palgrave and William Allingham, and the sculptor Thomas Woolner. Tennyson's last companion was his own son, Hallam.

## 1861

The Prince Consort died.

## 1862

**March:** Tennyson was invited to visit the Queen at Osborne. Queen Victoria derived great comfort from reading *In Memoriam* after the death of her husband and although Tennyson and Queen Victoria could never be close friends they held each other in high regard. They met only half a dozen times but maintained an affectionate correspondence for the rest of Tennyson's life.

## 1864

**August:** *Enoch Arden* was published. More than 40,000 copies were sold within a short time of publication, overall making it Tennyson's most popular work in his own lifetime.

## 1865

**January:** Tennyson refused a baronetcy.
Tennyson accepted an invitation to become a Fellow of The Royal Society, having declined a previous invitation in 1864.
**February:** Tennyson's mother, Elizabeth Tennyson, died.

## 1867

As Tennyson's reputation grew Farringford was besieged by visitors and sightseers, and Tennyson began to look for a second home. He eventually decided to buy land near Haslemere on the Surrey/Sussex border.

## 1868

**23 April:** The foundation stone for Aldworth, the new house, was laid. It was intended as a summer cottage but, in fact, became a rather grand house with a pleasant domestic interior, designed by James Knowles, an architect who, encouragingly for Tennyson, shared an interest in Arthurian legends.

## 1869

**April:** Knowles persuaded Tennyson to be a founder of the Metaphysical Society: though he attended eleven meetings in ten years, he never formally spoke to his distinguished colleagues (once, in Tennyson's absence, Knowles read *The Higher Pantheon*, not a major contribution to speculative thought).
**Summer:** The family moved into their new home, at Aldworth.
**December:** *The Holy Grail and other poems* appeared, although the title page is dated 1870. It was published by Alexander Strahan with whom Tennyson had negotiated a very favourable five-year contract the previous year.

## 1872

*Idylls of the King* was published in what was almost its final form *(Balin and Balan* being added in 1874). The completed work had been written over a period of nearly forty years.

## 1873

Strahan could no longer honour his contract with Tennyson who immediately negotiated a contract with Henry S. King which guaranteed him £25,000 over the next five years.

**30 March:** Tennyson again declined the offer of a baronetcy. The offer was renewed the following year and was again refused.

## 1874

**Autumn:** Emily Tennyson suffered a total collapse in health after returning from a trip to France. Tennyson decided to recall Hallam from Cambridge University and from then on Hallam acted as his father's secretary, travelling companion and general factotum, submerging his own life in that of his father.

## 1875

**June:** *Queen Mary: a drama* was published, Tennyson's first attempt as a playwright. In 1874, after seeing Henry Irving as Hamlet, he decided to write dramatic works, which henceforth were a major preoccupation. Over the next ten years he wrote a number of plays, none of which were particularly successful.

## 1876

**18 April:** *Queen Mary* opened at the Lyceum with an audience largely composed of Tennyson's friends. The production was not a success and was withdrawn after 23 performances.

**September:** Tennyson and Hallam went to visit one of his oldest friends, Edward Fitzgerald.

**December:** *Harold,* Tennyson's second play, was published, but because of the lack of success of *Queen Mary* it was not produced on the stage until a decade later.

## 1878

**February:** Lionel Tennyson married Eleanor Locker in Westminster Abbey.

## 1879

Tennyson finished the writing of his next play *Becket*, which he submitted to Irving for production. However, it was so long that it was financially impossible to produce at that time.

**April:** Tennyson's brother Charles Tennyson Turner died.

**December:** *The Falcon* was produced at St. James's Theatre, where it ran for 67 performances.

## 1881

**March:** Throughout the 1870s and 1880s Tennyson lost many of his friends and contemporaries and in March of this year one of his oldest friends, James Spedding, died.

**July:** Henry Irving and Ellen Terry appeared in Tennyson's play *The Cup* at the Lyceum.

## 1882

**November:** Tennyson's last play, *The Promise of May,* his only prose work, opened at the Globe Theatre. The play was a total failure. Although Tennyson was bitterly disappointed with his lack of success in the theatre, the failures did no real harm to his reputation.

## 1883

**December:** Tennyson finally agreed to accept a barony. The title he chose was Baron Tennyson of Aldworth and Freshwater.

## 1884

**15 January:** Tennyson signed a ten-year contract with Alexander Macmillan with a minimum guarantee of £1,500 annually.

**11 March:** Tennyson took his seat in the House of Lords.

## 1884

**June:** Hallam Tennyson and Audrey Boyle were married in Westminster Abbey.

## 1885

**November:** *Tiresias and other Poems,* dedicated to Robert Browning, was published. Most of the poems had already appeared elsewhere but the new volume was regarded as a major event and attracted many favourable reviews.

## 1886

**20 April:** At the age of 32 Lionel Tennyson died on board ship whilst returning from India.

## 1888

**September:** Tennyson suffered an attack of severe rheumatic gout, his most serious illness to date.

## 1889

**August:** Tennyson's eightieth birthday brought hundreds of letters and telegrams in tribute.

**October:** Tennyson wrote 'Crossing the Bar', an extempore effusion which he asked Hallam to put 'at the end of all editions of my poems'.

## 1892

**December:** *Demeter and other Poems* was published, selling 20,000 copies within the first week.

**March:** Tennyson's play *The Foresters* was produced in New York.

**April:** Irving agreed to produce *Becket*, which was staged in February 1893 with Sir Henry Irving and Ellen Terry in the leading roles, and with the music composed by Charles Villiers Stanford. Bram Stoker was the business manager. This posthumous production became the most commercially successful of all Tennyson's plays - the text being freely cut by Irving to almost half its length.

**July:** At the end of the month Tennyson caught a slight cold which was the start of his final illness.

**6 October:** Tennyson died at Aldworth in the early hours of the morning with his family at his bedside.

**12 October:** Tennyson's funeral took place in Westminster Abbey, the service being conducted by the Dean of Westminster. Emily Tennyson was too weak to attend but the Abbey was crowded for the occasion and there were huge crowds waiting outside.

**28 October:** Posthumous publication of *The Death of Oenone, Akbar's Dream and other Poems*.

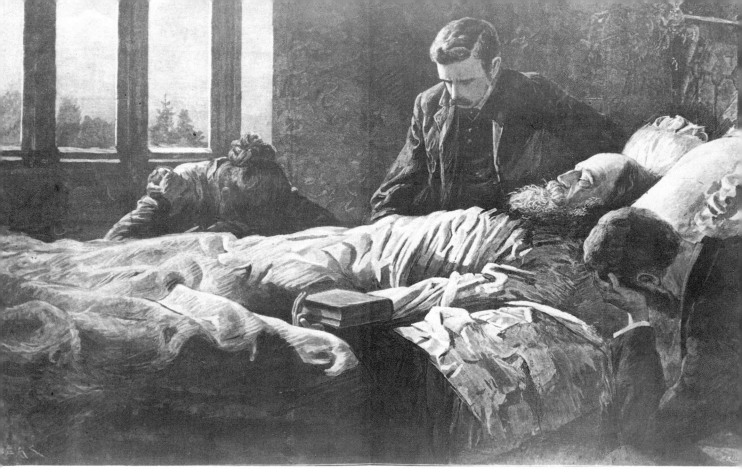

Cat. 2

# 1. Death of a Poet

When Tennyson died one hundred years ago this year, on 6 October 1892, it was a national event. Tennyson at his death was more than the most popular poet since Byron; he had become, not entirely willingly, a public figure and a spokesman for his age. A *Times* editorial earlier in the year had proclaimed him a more valuable national asset than the greatest statesman of the Victorian period, W.E. Gladstone:

We have one Grand Old Man in England who is greater than even Mr Gladstone. He is older than Mr Gladstone, and a much older Liberal. When Mr Gladstone was a Tory Lord Tennyson was putting his Liberal politics into the most exquisite poetry. When Mr Gladstone's golden voice ceases to be heard by his countrymen only historical students will search to discover the secret of the magic of his eloquence. Lord Tennyson is immortal. He is as much above Mr Gladstone as Shakspere is above the Cecil who conducted the work of statesmanship under Queen Elizabeth. Lord Tennyson, in every candid man's opinion, is our greatest living man. He is an old friend of Mr Gladstone's. The two have journeyed together in recent years. Their regard for each other is even pathetic. We look back to Mr Gladstone's criticism of Lord Tennyson's "Maud" as, perhaps, the finest example which it is possible to produce of the politician dealing justly with the poet. Lord Tennyson is no mere dreamer. He is a practical man. What is his judgement upon the present controversy? His genius for style has caused him to produce the finest saying which

has been elaborated since the speeches began over the General Election. His letter has all the force of an epigram. It will be an historic letter. Tennyson is the Shakspere of our day. Nothing that he utters will die. We therefore emphasise as far as we can his proclamation of opinion. Here it is in full. "June 28. Sir, - I love Mr Gladstone, but hate his present Irish policy. - I am, yours faithfully, Tennyson." Lord Tennyson has nothing to induce him to become partisan. He is not, in the true sense, a partisan at all. He is only one amongst all the men of genius of our time, amongst all the leaders, whether in poetic achievement, science, or art, who reject Mr Gladstone's policy. He condemns it with the strongest word he could use. He "hates" it.

Six days after Tennyson's death, Churchwarden Edmund Barnes (Mayor of St. Pancras 1900-1903),speaking to the Vestry of St Pancras, used the following words:

Few men are really great; few men are really great and good. It is because the Poet Laureate was so good and so great that his name is revered throughout the world. . . Great indeed was he - head and shoulders above the poets of the present age A born poet he has lived a long, active and honoured life, and has gone down to the grave honoured and revered by us all. The nation has today honoured itself by honouring this great and good man. Truly this was a life that might be copied in every particular by all of us, aye, and by those who come after us. We have suffered indeed a national loss and if his death be a loss to the nation, what must it be to those nearest and dearest to him.

For the Victorians, and for the following generation, Tennyson was a great poet because he was a great man, a model of moral excellence. In James Joyce's *A Portrait of the Artist as a Young Man* (1916), Stephen Dedalus earns the abuse of his companions by comparing him unfavourably with the immoral Byron:

- And who is the best poet, Heron? asked Boland.
- Lord Tennyson, of course, answered Heron.
- O, yes, Lord Tennyson, said Nash. We have all his poetry at home in a book.

At this Stephen forgot the silent vows he had been making and burst out:

- Tennyson a poet! Why, he's only a rhymester!
- O, get out! said Heron. Everyone knows that Tennyson is the greatest poet.
- And who do you think is the greatest poet? asked Boland, nudging his neighbour.
- Byron, of course, answered Stephen.

Heron gave the lead and all three joined in a scornful laugh.

- What are you laughing at? asked Stephen.
- You, said Heron. Byron the greatest poet! He's only a poet for uneducated people.
- He must be a fine poet! said Boland.
- You may keep your mouth shut, said Stephen, turning on him boldly. All you know about poetry is what you wrote up on the slates in the yard and were going to be sent to the loft for.

Boland, in fact, was said to have written on the slates in the yard a couplet about a classmate of his who often rode home from the college on a pony:

> *As Tyson was riding into Jerusalem*
> *He fell and hurt his Alec Kafoozelum.*

This thrust put the two lieutenants to silence but Heron went on:

- In any case Byron was a heretic and immoral too.
- I don't care what he was, cried Stephen hotly.
- You don't care whether he was a heretic or not? said Nash.
- What do you know about it? shouted Stephen. You never read a line of anything in your life except a trans or Boland either.
- I know that Byron was a bad man, said Boland.
- Here, catch hold of this heretic, Heron called out.

In a moment Stephen was a prisoner.[1]

To the young James Joyce, at the end of the nineteenth century, Tennyson was the father-figure against whom it was natural to revolt. Now, one hundred years after Tennyson's death, we do not seek to express his greatest qualities as a poet simply in terms of his morality. Indeed, where he shows good sense, good-heartedness and natural courtesy, as he does in the *Idylls of the King*, we decide that most of these poems are more pleasing than powerful. When Stephen Dedalus scorns Tennyson as a 'rhymester' he does in fact point to his real vitality. The poet who said he could scan

every word in English except perhaps the word 'scissors' had an awesome technical skill. In 1936 T.S. Eliot published his timely and apt salute:

In ending we must go back to the beginning and remember that *In Memoriam* would not be a great poem, or Tennyson a great poet, without the technical accomplishment. Tennyson is the great master of metric as well as of melancholia; I do not think any poet in English has ever had a finer ear for vowel sound as well as a subtler feeling for some moods of anguish . . . And this technical gift of Tennyson's is no slight thing. Tennyson lived in a time which was already acutely time-conscious: a great many things seemed to be happening, railways were being built, discoveries were being made, the face of the world was changing. That was a time busy in keeping up to date. It had, for the most part, no hold on permanent things, on permanent truths about man and God and life and death. The surface of Tennyson stirred about with his time; and he had nothing to which to hold fast except his unique and unerring feeling for the sounds of words. But in this he had something that no one else had. Tennyson's surface, his technical accomplishment, is intimate with his depths: what we most quickly see about Tennyson is that which moves between the surface and the depths, that which is of slight importance. By looking innocently at the surface we are most likely to come to the depths, to the abyss of sorrow. Tennyson is not only a minor Virgil, he is also with Virgil as Dante saw him, a Virgil among the Shades, the saddest of all English poets, among the Great in Limbo, the most instinctive rebel against the society in which he was the most perfect conformist.

Tennyson seems to have reached the end of his spiritual development with *In Memoriam*; there followed no reconciliation, no resolution.

> And now no sacred staff shall break in blossom,
> No choral salutation lure to light
> A spirit sick with perfume and sweet night,

or rather with twilight, for Tennyson faced neither the darkness nor the light in his later years. The genius, the technical power, persisted to the end, but the spirit had surrendered. A gloomier end than that of Baudelaire: Tennyson had no *singulier avertissement*. And having turned aside from the journey through the dark night, to become the surface flatterer of his own time, he has been rewarded with the despite of an age that succeeds his own in shallowness.[2]

This is finely suggestive, a poet's criticism, but Eliot is a little too harsh on the writing after *In Memoriam*. In *Maud* Tennyson showed that he was still alive to trying new forms, to writing experimentally. The terrors of love and the ecstasy of desire rise dramatically in that poem out of an intensely dark drive towards death. And there is a full, social, contemporary background. Tennyson is certainly no 'minor Virgil' here; he is himself, and still giving us good reason to celebrate his life and work, as we do here in this exhibition.

# Last illness

**1**

**Bulletin announcing Tennyson's death**
October 6, 1892
Lincolnshire County Council:
Tennyson Research Centre, Lincoln

The bulletin, placed outside Tennyson's home, reads: 'Lord Tennyson passed away quite peacefully at 1.35 A.M. Signed Andrew Clark George H.R. Dabbs October 6 1892'.

Sir Andrew Clark refused a prior engagement with the Shah of Persia to attend to Tennyson, a choice that pleased the Shah, who conferred upon him the Persian Order of the Lion and the Sun. Dabbs was Tennyson's doctor from the Isle of Wight.

**2**

**Tennyson on his deathbed**
Unknown artist
1892
Photograph 28.1 x 45 cms
Lincolnshire County Council:
Tennyson Research Centre, Lincoln

Tennyson lies on the bed, Shakespeare's works in his hand, with his son Hallam, daughter-in-law Audrey and the medical attendant Dr. Dabbs. Inscribed below, 'The Death of Lord Tennyson'.

**3**

**Audrey, Lady Tennyson**
Notebook entitled *Illness Etc*
1892
Lincolnshire County Council:
Tennyson Research Centre, Lincoln

At her husband's request, Audrey Tennyson recorded Tennyson's last moments in minute detail. The close, factual notes were to assist Hallam when he came to write his *Memoir* of his father.

12-57 We again thought the dear spirit was passing home & D^r Dabbs looked at his watch & said he thought his long journey must be near its end but again the pulse revived till 1-25 when several spasmodic gasps came followed by long silences & D^r Dabbs could feel no more pulse and Hallam said "I can only say his own words "God accept him Christ receive him, and both nurses fell on their knees in prayer & I thought of his Lionel my father, Mordie, Harry & Eleanor all welcoming the one we so loved in their Heavenly Home, all in a solemn silence and then Hallam asked "is it over" & D^r Dabbs said "I think there is one more breath to come and then after what seemed a long silence came a little sharp, short breath at 1-35 am by D^r Dabb's watch, and our darling had entered his Eternal Home & we rose & left him in the moonlit room.

# Funeral

**4**

**J. Walter**
Funeral of Tennyson in Westminster Abbey
1892
Print from wood engraving 50.5 x 34 cms
Lincolnshire County Council:
Tennyson Research Centre, Lincoln

From the *Illustrated London News*, 15 October 1892. Emily Tennyson wrote to the Dean of Westminster: 'Decide as you think best. If it is thought better, let him have the flag of England on his coffin . . . let the flag represent the feelings of the beloved Queen, and the nation, and the empire he loved so dearly.'

For Hallam, who saw his father as the moral spokesman for his countrymen, the state funeral at Westminster Abbey seemed a perfect conclusion:

The Abbey was crowded from end to end by a vast multitude of mourners. The nave was lined by men of the Balaclava Light Brigade, by some of the London Rifle Volunteers, and by the boys of the Gordon Boys Home, in token of their gratitude for what he had done for each and all of them. . . . Nothing can have been more simple and majestic than the funeral service: and the tributes of sympathy which we received from many countries and from all creeds and classes were not only remarkable for their universality, but for their depth of feeling.[3]

**5**

**Card of admission to Tennyson's funeral**
1892
Lincolnshire County Council:
Tennyson Research Centre, Lincoln

For others, however, the funeral seemed to detract attention away from Tennyson's real achievement, the great poetry, and concentrate on the later, public persona: 'a lovely day,' wrote Henry James, 'the Abbey looked beautiful, everyone was there, but something - I don't know what - of real impressiveness - was wanting . . . too many masters of Balliol, too many Deans and Alfred Austins'[4]. Austin became Poet Laureate in 1896.

**6**

**Unknown artist**
Digging Tennyson's grave in Westminster Abbey
1892
Photograph from drawing 46 x 34 cms
Lincolnshire County Council:
Tennyson Research Centre, Lincoln

From the *Illustrated London News*. Tennyson was buried in Poets' Corner, next to Robert Browning and in front of the Chaucer monument.

Cat. 4

## Memorials

**7**

**Unknown artist**
G.F. Watts at work on the Tennyson Statue
1892
Photograph 40 x 29.5 cms
The Watts Gallery

Cat. 7

**8**

**Casts of 'Tennyson's head' for the Tennyson Statue**
George Frederic Watts
The Watts Gallery

George Frederic Watts (1817-1904) was the son of a Hereford piano manufacturer who had moved to London. In both painting and sculpture he showed an interest in allegorical subjects; and allegory is not absent from his portraits, about one hundred in number. Some of his finest oils relate to Tennyson and his family, and the massive statue he completed in 1903, now outside Lincoln cathedral, is his final tribute to the poet.

That the bronze statue is 'larger than life' is one of Watts's attempts to find a way of paying tribute to a certain spiritual quality which he found in the poet's work. He knew him personally because both were friends of Julia Margaret Cameron and a part of the intellectual circle on the Isle of Wight. This personal knowledge is reflected in the statue, including the image of Tennyson's much-beloved dog Karenina, a Russian wolfhound, but the idealising of the figure as a bowed, prophetic and cloaked presence relates to earlier images. These often have a brilliant, celebratory colour, depicting the poet and his family with both admiration and delight. The portraits of Emily and of the two boys, Hallam and Lionel, lack such symbolic patterning as the bay leaves which surround Tennyson's head in the 'moonlight portrait'. Indeed, that icon has suggestions of sanctity, a pensive, even Christ-like man, all wrinkles removed, the beard more kempt than the photographs allow.

**9**

**Address from a General Meeting of the Vestry of St Pancras**
[12 October] 1892
Lincolnshire County Council:
Tennyson Research Centre, Lincoln

The address conveys a message of condolence to Lady Tennyson and the Tennyson family:

St Pancras, London.

At a General Meeting of the Vestry held at the Vestry Hall, on Wednesday the 12th day of October 1892, Mr. Churchwarden Purchese in the Chair; and seventy-eight other members present. It was Moved by Mr. Churchwarden Barnes, Seconded by Mr. Bryant, and Resolved Unanimously. That this Vestry being the municiple authority for one of the largest Districts of the Metropolis, containing a population of about 250,000 Inhabitants, do hereby record their deep regret on the death of Lord Tennyson, the Poet Laureate, and with the Inhabitants of the Parish generally, join in the universal appreciation of the lofty and generous character of this one of England's greatest Sons, and do convey to Lady Tennyson, and the Family of the deceased Nobleman, the deepest sympathy of the Vestry and the Parishioners generally with them in their sad bereavement.

The Common Seal of the Vestry of the Parish of S[t] Pancras in the County of London affixed hereto by order.

**10**

**Wreath presented by Queen Victoria**
Lincolnshire County Council:
Tennyson Research Centre, Lincoln

Tennyson's good relationship with Queen Victoria is well-known. This wreath has a card attached, in the Queen's hand, which reads: 'A tribute of affectionate regard and true admiration from his Sovereign'.

11

**A selection of Tennyson personalia**
Lincolnshire County Council:
Tennyson Research Centre, Lincoln

Many of the poet's everyday possessions were carefully preserved, including those objects connected with his death.

1.  Writing desk
2.  Pruning Knife
3.  Scissors
4.  Fruit knife
5.  Watches
6.  Silver tankard, 'Presented to the Right Honourable the Lord Tennyson by Spiers and Pond, Ltd., on the closing of the Cock Tavern, Fleet Street, 1886'.
7.  Chess set
8.  Wood carving of ivy leaves made by Tennyson for casting in plaster
9.  Umbrella, with engraved plate 'A. Tennyson, Aldworth, Haslemere, and walking stick
10. Brush and comb
11. Pearls worn by Tennyson's mother
12. Ticket for the International exhibition
13. Bead purse made by Elizabeth Fytche, the poet's mother
14. Card case
15. Card case
16. Child's gloves
17. Dog Whistle
18. Hat
19. Engraved silver snuff box belonging Sir John Franklin
20. Medicine box, with label, 'Last medicine and drop glass used by him and for him Oct^ber 6th 1892'.
21. Pipes
22. Bottle that contained eau de cologne used to clean Tennyson's pipes
23. Durham Smoking Mixture, given to Tennyson by an American admirer
24. Binoculars in leather case, engraved 'Alfred Tennyson from Sabine Greville, 1887'.
25. Spectacles and cases
26. Pocket microscope
27. Thermometer used during the poet's last illness
28. Lenses
29. Quills
30. Pencil and pen
31. Bronze medallion of Henry Hallam, historian and father of Arthur Hallam
32. Cameo of Tennyson
33. Cameo of Tennyson
34. Bronze medallion of Tennyson
35. Bronze medal awarded to Tennyson at the 1862 Exhibition
36. Bronze medallion of Tennyson
37. Watercolour paint box, with six colours and brush
38. Cloak, *c.*1840, worn until 1870, when it was given with hat (39) to Frederick Locker
39. A travelling hat given to Locker

## Cartoons

12

**Max Beerbohm (1872-1956)**
*Mr Tennyson reading 'In Memoriam' to his Sovereign*
1904
Print 20 x 32 cms
Lincolnshire County Council:
Tennyson Research Centre, Lincoln

After an exhibition at the Carfax Gallery run by Robert Ross in Rider Street, London, Max Beerbohm published a series of aesthetic cartoons commenting on writers, dead and alive, under the title *The Poets' Corner*.

Tennyson was famous for his readings of his own poetry, and for his personal rapport with Queen Victoria. He and the Queen are two diminutive figures, set in a brilliance of crimson, yellow and turquoise. Beerbohm's view, stated in 1899 in *The Spirit of Caricature*, was that 'Caricature never has had moral influence of any kind.' His work purposes to be 'beautiful' and, at the same time, miniature in scale, working with affection against the inflated and the pretentious. Beerbohm writes:

The most perfect caricature is that which, on a small surface, with the simplest means most accurately exaggerates, to the highest point, the peculiarities of a human being, and his most beautiful manner.[5]

Compared with Beerbohm, even Pellegrini, the cartoonist 'Ape' in the magazine *Vanity Fair,* lacks wit, spontaneity and the sheer surprise of mischievous anecdote. Beerbohm's caption is essential to his conception.

13

**Carlo Pellegrini or 'Ape' (1839-1889)**
*Men of the Day No. 28 "The Poet Laureate"*
1871
Print 31.5 x 19 cms
The Wordsworth Trust

From 1869 Pellegrini published several hundred caricatures of statesmen and other famous men of the day in the magazine *Vanity Fair,* nearly all drawn from memory.

14

**Unknown artist**
*Alfred Tennyson the Laureate of King Arthur*
1870
Newspaper print 32 x 27.5 cms
Lincolnshire County Council:
Tennyson Research Centre, Lincoln

A cartoon from *Punch*, Saturday 1 January 1870.

# 2. Tennyson Portraits

The Victorian cult of hero worship finds expression in the extraordinary number of images available of the famous men of the time. The commissioned portrait was supplemented by the informal sketch, the caricature, and, particularly, the photograph, which added a new dimension to portraiture.

From the rare, romanticised portraits of the younger Tennyson, one moves to the inventive photographic images, and then to a series of late drawings and paintings that can seem too dependent on the photographs.

**15**

**Alfred Lord Tennyson**
Portrait by Anne Weld
*c.*1830
Pencil 16.4 x 12 cms
Lincolnshire County Council:
Tennyson Research Centre, Lincoln

The artist, married to Charles Weld, was born Anne Sellwood, sister to Emily who became Tennyson's wife. Robert Martin's recent redating would make this the earliest known portrait of Tennyson, and probably contemporary with Anne Weld's sketch of Arthur Hallam - this last drawing hung above Tennyson's fireplace for the rest of his life.

**16**

**Alfred Lord Tennyson**
Portrait by J.H. Lynch after Samuel Laurence
*c.*1839
Lithograph 31 x 23.7 cms
Spedding Collection

Two months after Tennyson's death the artist Edward Burne-Jones was asked by Hallam Tennyson and Lady Tennyson to repaint the portrait of the poet by Samuel Laurence, given to the Tennysons by his friend Edward Fitzgerald. Early prints such as this one of the untouched Laurence suggest that Burne-Jones softened the expression and made the overall tone more conventional.

**17**

**Alfred Lord Tennyson**
Portrait possibly by Samuel Laurence
No date
Oil on canvas 85.5 x 72 cms
Mr John Moxon Collection

This is the version of the Samuel Laurence portrait which hung behind Edward Moxon's chair. The differences between it and the original could again be attributed to the later alterations by Burne-Jones. The portrait is unfortunately bituminised.

**18**

**Alfred Lord Tennyson**
Portrait by Thomas Woolner
1850
Bronze medallion D 29.5 cms
Lincolnshire County Council:
Tennyson Research Centre, Lincoln

Tennyson sat for the medallion in 1849, when Woolner was still struggling as an artist. He was an unreliable sitter, and Woolner only managed to complete the portrait when, in 1850, he tracked Tennyson down to Tent Lodge, Coniston, where the poet was spending his honeymoon.

**19**

**Alfred Lord Tennyson**
Portrait by James Mudd
1857
Photograph: albumen print 8 x 6.5 cms
Lincolnshire County Council:
Tennyson Research Centre, Lincoln

Published in *Poets in the Pulpit*, edited by H.R. Haweis (London, 1880). The portrait was taken at Manchester, during the National Art Exhibition. Nathaniel Hawthorne has left a description of Tennyson's appearance at the event:

The most picturesque figure without affectation that I ever saw, of middle size, rather slouching, dressed entirely in black and nothing white about him except the collar of his shirt, which methought might have been clean the day before. He had on a black wideawake hat, with round crown and wide irregular brim, beneath which came down his long black hair, looking terribly tangled; he had a long pointed beard, too, a little browner than the hair, and not so abundant as to encumber any of the expression of his face. His frock coat was buttoned accross his breast though the afternoon was warm. His face was very dark, and not exactly a smooth face, but worn, and expressing great sensitiveness. . . .[6]

Mudd of Manchester was a well-known photographer, but examples of portraiture in his work are relatively rare.

**20**

**Alfred Lord Tennyson**
Portrait by J.E. Mayall
1864
Photograph 11 x 7.5 cms
Lincolnshire County Council:
Tennyson Research Centre, Lincoln

**21**
**Alfred Lord Tennyson**
Portrait by J.E. Mayall
1864
Coloured miniature of original photograph
8 x 6.4 cms
Lincolnshire County Council:
Tennyson Research Centre, Lincoln

Tennyson's favourite image of himself, closely followed by 'The Dirty Monk' portrait by Julia Margaret Cameron.

Cat. 21

**22**
**Alfred Lord Tennyson**
Portrait by Julia Margaret Cameron
1865
Photograph 25.2 x 20.4 cms
Lincolnshire County Council:
Tennyson Research Centre, Lincoln

'The Dirty Monk' portrait. Inscribed below are the words: 'I prefer The Dirty Monk to the others of me. A Tennyson. Except one by Mayall'. The artist was unimpressed by this remark. In her unfinished manuscript, *Annals of My Glass House* (1874), she wrote:

Meanwhile I took another immortal head, that of Alfred Tennyson, and the result was that profile portrait which he himself designates as the "Dirty Monk." It is a fit representation of Isaiah or of Jeremiah, and Henry Taylor said the picture was as fine as Alfred Tennyson's finest poem. The Laureate has since said of it that he likes it better than any photograph that has been taken of him *except* one by Mayall, that *"except"* speaks for

itself. The comparison seems too comical. It is rather like comparing one of Madame Toussaud's waxwork heads to one of Woolner's ideal heroic busts.[7]

**23**
**Alfred Lord Tennyson**
By Thomas Woolner
1866
Marble relief sculpture 34.5 x 34.5 cms
Lincolnshire County Council:
Tennyson Research Centre, Lincoln

Woolner worked on this occasion not from life, but from photographs taken of Tennyson, under his direction, at the London Stereoscopic Company on 29 November 1864.

**24**
**Alfred Lord Tennyson**
Portrait by Julia Margaret Cameron
1867
Photograph 35.1 x 26.5 cms
Lincolnshire County Council:
Tennyson Research Centre, Lincoln

Tennyson sat for Julia Margaret Cameron on at least seven occasions. Considering the length of exposure, typically anything from three to seven minutes, this was no small ordeal (described by Carlyle as an 'inferno'), and it is an indication of both the affection he had for Mrs Cameron and the esteem in which he held her work. But he did resent the public recognition that the portraits brought him, on one occasion complaining to her, 'I can't be anonymous by reason of your confounded photographs'.

**25**
**Alfred Lord Tennyson**
Portrait by Julia Margaret Cameron
1867
Carbon print 33.4 x 25.2 cms
Lincolnshire County Council:
Tennyson Research Centre, Lincoln

A later, commercial printing of the above portrait, using a red tint.

**26**
**Alfred Lord Tennyson**
Portrait by Julia Margaret Cameron
1869
Photograph: albumen print 28.9 x 24.8 cms
National Portrait Gallery, London

Emily Tennyson writes in her journal for 2 June 1869, 'A. is photographed by Mrs. Cameron. One of the portraits majestic but lacking delicacy.'[8]

Cat. 28

Cat. 29

**27**

**Alfred Lord Tennyson**
Portrait by Ernest Gustave Girardot
*c.*1869
Oil on canvas 56 x 47 cms
Lincolnshire County Council:
Tennyson Research Centre, Lincoln

A painting based on the Mayall photograph.

**28**

**Alfred Lord Tennyson**
Portrait by Benjamin Scott of Carlisle
1871
Photograph: platinotype 24.5 x 32 cms
Lincolnshire County Council:
Tennyson Research Centre, Lincoln

In September 1871 Tennyson went to visit George James Howard, later the 9th Earl of Carlisle, at Naworth Castle. Lady St Helier was an admiring fellow guest:

I well remember the excitement with which I sat down to listen to him, and the increasing delight with which I heard him pour out the impassioned words of "Maud" in his wonderful sonorous voice, with its deep vibration and all its endless shades of expression. If I remember rightly, he read it straight through, and then shut the book without a word. The only evidence of the intensity of feeling which he threw into it was the way in which he seized, twisted, and pulled about a large brocade cushion which lay beside him on the sofa, while we sitting round him hardly dared to give expression to the profound emotions with which we had listened to that wonderful music.[9]

**29**

**Alfred Lord Tennyson**
Portrait by George James Howard, 9th Earl of Carlisle
1871
Pencil 23 x 36.5 cms
Lord Henley Collection

Probably done during Tennyson's visit to Naworth Castle. George Howard was a skilled amateur artist, and was friendly with Edward Burne-Jones, George Frederic Watts and Sir Charles Holroyd.

**30**

**Alfred Lord Tennyson**
By Thomas Woolner
1876
Marble bust 67 x 43 x 30 cms
Lincolnshire County Council:
Tennyson Research Centre, Lincoln

The 'bearded bust' was sculpted by Woolner in 1873. Hallam reports in his diary that his father was 'daily at Mr. Woolner's studio because of the new sittings'. Woolner was, by now, a very successful portrait sculptor and a personal friend of Tennyson, and so he had no trouble in obtaining him for sittings. It can be compared with an earlier bust, unbearded, from 1857, which is now at Trinity College, Cambridge.

**31**

**Alfred Lord Tennyson**
Portrait by Sir Hubert von Herkomer
1879
Charcoal 88 x 52 cms
Lincolnshire County Council:
Tennyson Research Centre, Lincoln

**32**

**Alfred Lord Tennyson**
Portrait by Frederick Sandys
Signed and dated 1884
Coloured chalks 67.3 x 50.2 cms
The Earl of Stockton and the Macmillan Family Trustees

Frederick Sandys (1829-1904) was closely associated with the artists, poets and writers of the Pre-Raphaelite school. From an early period he was well-known for his brilliant crayon portraits, and in 1880 received a commission from Messrs. Macmillan & Co. for a series of literary portraits, which include Robert Browning, Matthew Arnold, and this rarely seen image of Tennyson.

**33**

**Alfred Lord Tennyson**
Portrait by George Barnett Smith
1885
Etching 22.3 x 14 cms
Lincolnshire County Council:
Tennyson Research Centre, Lincoln

**34**

**Alfred Lord Tennyson**
Portrait by William Barraud
October 1888
Photograph 37 x 27 cms
Lincolnshire County Council:
Tennyson Research Centre, Lincoln

**35**

**Alfred Lord Tennyson**
Portrait by William Henry Margetson
Signed with initials, 1891
Watercolour 32.7 x 24.1 cms
National Portrait Gallery, London

Margetson has based his portrait on the Barraud photograph.

36

**Alfred Lord Tennyson**
Portrait by George Frederic Watts
Signed and dated 1890
Red pastel 53.5 x 40.5 cms
Lincolnshire County Council:
Tennyson Research Centre, Lincoln

In August 1890, Watts was asked by Hallam
Tennyson for a red or black chalk drawing to serve
as a frontispiece to the new Macmillan Popular
Edition of Tennyson's poems. The sketch is based
upon portraits of the poet done by Watts earlier in
the year. It was described by Emily Tennyson as
'magnificent and most pathetic', and was hung in
the library at Aldworth, Tennyson's Sussex home.

37

**Alfred Lord Tennyson**
Portrait possibly by Barruad
No date
Photograph 53.5 x 66.3 cms
Lincolnshire County Council:
Tennyson Research Centre, Lincoln

38

**Alfred Lord Tennyson**
Portrait by unknown artist
No date
Photograph 21 x 14 cms
Dorothy Milnes Collection

39

**Alfred Lord Tennyson**
Portrait by Lowes Dickinson
1892
Pencil and chalk 42 x 35.5 cms
Lincolnshire County Council:
Tennyson Research Centre, Lincoln

Lowes Dickinson has based his portrait on the
Mayall photograph.

40

**Alfred Lord Tennyson**
By Francis John Williamson
1893
Plaster 86 x 58 x 36 cms
Lincolnshire County Council:
Tennyson Research Centre, Lincoln

Like the Watts statue outside Lincoln Cathedral,
Williamson's bust is of monumental size, and its
physical presence is deliberately imposing.

Cat. 52

Cat. 53

# 3. Early Life

## Family

Tennyson grew up under the constant threat of poverty and violence. Often drunk and always paranoid, his father never recovered from being disinherited in favour of his younger brother. On top of this, he suffered from epilepsy and melancholia, and Tennyson, who watched two of his brothers also descend into madness, was at times convinced that he too had inherited 'the black bloodedness of the Tennysons.'

**41**

**George Tennyson (1750-1835)**
Portrait by Sir Thomas Lawrence
No date
Oil on canvas 75 x 61.5 cms
Lincolnshire County Council:
Tennyson Research Centre, Lincoln

The poet's grandfather. His early career was as a solicitor in Market Rasen, but as his wealth and landed property increased he settled into the role of country gentleman. He considered Charles, the younger of his two sons, the most suitable as an heir, and so, in an act that was to disturb many people's peace of mind, he disinherited his eldest son George Clayton, Tennyson's father.

George Tennyson was a successful, self-made man. When Tennyson wrote a poem on his grandmother's death his grandfather gave him half a guinea, but with a warning: 'Here is half a guinea for you, the first you have ever earned by poetry, and take my word for it, the last.'[10]

**42**

**Mary Tennyson, née Turner (1753-1825)**
Portrait by John Russell
1805
Pastel painting 74 x 61 cms
Lincolnshire County Council:
Tennyson Research Centre, Lincoln

The poet's grandmother. She seems to have had some sensitivity for poetry, unlike her husband, and unlike her brother Charles. Hallam Tennyson writes in his *Memoir*:

[She] would assert: 'Alfred's poetry all comes from me." My father remembered her reading to him, when a boy, "The Prisoner of Chillon" very tenderly. Sam Turner [her brother], on the contrary, smashed the bottom out of his glass of rum and water on the dinner table, as he inveighed against "this new-fangled Byron."[11]

The portrait is by John Russell (1745-1806), a Royal Academician famous for his portraits in coloured crayons. In the distance is Bayons Manor, the family home in Lincolnshire.

**43**

**Elizabeth Russell, née Tennyson (1776-c.1866)**
Portrait by John Russell
1805
Pastel painting 74 x 62 cms
Lincolnshire County Council:
Tennyson Research Centre, Lincoln

Tennyson's aunt, also painted by John Russell. She was the wife of Matthew Russell, one of the richest men in England, and lived in splendour at Brancepeth Castle in County Durham. One of Tennyson's strongest supporters, she provided him with an annual allowance of £100, from his Cambridge days up until his marriage in 1850.

**44**

**George Clayton Tennyson (1778-1831)**
Portrait by unknown artist
c.1812
Oil on canvas 73 x 61 cms
Lincolnshire County Council:
Tennyson Research Centre, Lincoln

The poet's father. Tennyson loathed all forms of biographical enquiry, and was quiet about the most important figure in his early life. Similarly his son's *Memoir* is reticent about the extent of George Clayton Tennyson's mental and physical decay. But it is clear that Tennyson regarded him with both fear and affection, and the father-figure is a central presence in the early parts of *Maud*:

What! am I raging alone as my father raged in his mood?
Must *I* too creep to the hollow and dash myself down and die
Rather than hold by the law that I made, nevermore to brood
On a horror of shatter'd limbs and a wretched swindler's lie?
(*Maud*, 53-6)

**45**

**Elizabeth Tennyson, née Fytche (1781-1865)**
Portrait by unknown artist
No date
Watercolour H 8.6 cms
Lincolnshire County Council:
Tennyson Research Centre, Lincoln

**46**

**Elizabeth Tennyson, née Fytche**
Portrait by unknown artist
No date
Oil on canvas 49 x 49 cms
Lincolnshire County Council:
Tennyson Research Centre, Lincoln

Seemingly an amateur painting based on the original watercolour.

Tennyson's mother was described by Edward Fitzgerald as 'one of the most innocent and tender-hearted ladies I ever saw'. The heroine of Tennyson's early poem *Isabel* is apparently a faithful description of her.

> Eyes not down-dropt nor over bright, but fed
> With the clear-pointed flame of chastity,
> Clear, without heat, undying, tended by
> Pure vestal thoughts in the translucent fane
> Of her still spirit; locks not wide-dispread,
> Madonna-wise on either side her head;
> Sweet lips whereon perpetually did reign
> The summer calm of golden charity,
> Were fixèd shadows of thy fixèd mood,
> Reverèd Isabel, the crown and head,
> The stately flower of female fortitude,
> Of perfect wifehood and pure lowlihead.
> (*Isabel*, 1-12)

**47**
**[George Clayton Tennyson]**
Portrait attributed to Arthur Tennyson
No date
Pen and ink 16.6 x 11.4 cms
Lincolnshire County Council:
Tennyson Research Centre, Lincoln

**Cat. 47**

**48**
**Elizabeth Tennyson, née Fytche aged 80**
Portrait by unknown artist
*c.*1860
Coloured photograph H 14.5 cms
Lincolnshire County Council:
Tennyson Research Centre, Lincoln

Two portraits showing Tennyson's mother and father in later life. Their marriage cannot have been easy. Three remarkable letters, written between 1820 and 1829, illustrate how strained relations had become between husband and wife, as well as father and son.

**49**
**George Clayton Tennyson**
Letter to George Tennyson
14 August 1820
County Archives, Lincolnshire County Council

Mr Dear Father, I find to my great disquietude that you have thought proper to attribute to my suggestion or instigation certain expressions which may or may not have been used by Miss Fytche reflecting upon your conduct as a parent. I utterly disdain to exculpate myself from this charge. I did intend to have visited Tealby, but an accusation so unjust, so frequently reiterated and so totally unsubstantiated has so far oppress'd my spirits and irritated my feelings that it is impossible that I can do so with any pleasure - With the sentiments you yet entertain and have entertained for more than twenty years, I cannot wonder you told Mr. Bourne you had not a spark of affection for me. The rude and unprecedented manner in which you first address'd me at Hainton, after a long absence, on your return from York (I quote your own words "*Now you great awkward booby are you here*") holding me up to utter derision before Mr. Heneage, his sons & Sir Robt. Ainslie, & your language & conduct in innumerable other instances, many of which have made a deep impression upon my mind, sufficiently prove the truth of your own assertion - You have long injured me by your suspicions. I cannot avoid them for the fault is not mine. God judge between you & me - . You make and have always made a false estimate of me in every respect. You look and have always look'd upon me with a jaundiced eye, & *deeply and experimentally* feeling this, I am sure that my visiting you would not contribute to your satisfaction and at the same time would materially injure my own health and comfort. Conscious also that I am thrown into a situation unworthy my abilities & unbecoming either your fortune or my just pretensions, & resisted in every wish to promote my own interests or that of my family by removing to a more eligible situation, unaccountably kept in the dark with respect to their future prospects, with broken health & spirits, I find myself little disposed to encounter those unprovoked and sarcastic remarks in which you are so apt to indulge yourself at my expense, remarks, which tho' they may be outwardly borne, are inwardly resented, and prey upon the mind - the injustice, the inhumanity & the impropriety of which everyone can see but yourself, & which in your last visit were levelled against the father of a large family in the very presence of his children and that father between forty & fifty years of Age. I should not have proceeded thus far had you not by your unjust aspersions set fire to the Mass which was already disposed to ignite - You may forget or pass off as a jest what penetrates & rankles in my heart; you may break what is already bent, but there is a tribunal before which you and I may speedily appear, more speedily perhaps than either of us desire or expect - there it will be seen whether you through life have treated me with that consideration & kindness which a son has a right to expect from a father and whether (as you have been accustomed to represent me to myself & others) I have been deficient in filial affection & obedience

    I am, My dear Father
        your affectionate Son
            G.C. Tennyson

## 50

**George Tennyson**
Letter to Charles Tennyson d'Eyncourt
24 April 1822
County Archives, Lincolnshire County Council

My Dearest Chars

I have not got my post letters - today, probably there may be one from you; It hurt us much to hear of our dear little Georges late attack, we love that child & fear for him, we think you did right to leave him at Cheltenham, Will he be made happy there? It was lucky you left the place before your unbrotherly Bror arrived, I fear he will stir up much strife. I feel for our Dearest Eliza. Burn this letter . . .

## 51

**Elizabeth Tennyson, née Fytche**
Letter to George Tennyson
27 February 1829
County Archives, Lincolnshire County Council

My dear Sir

I am sorry to give you, or any one pain, but it is the extreme necessity of the case that urges me to express my most fixed and final resolution to separate from my husband as the only step that can effectually secure myself and family from the consequences of his ungovernable violence which I solemnly assure you has proceeded to such a length that I do not feel it safe either for myself or my children to remain any longer in the house with him. I understand from him that I have your sanction for this measure which even though it should not meet with your entire approbation, I know it to be absolutely necessary to our future comfort and tranquillity to adopt. Indeed Sir if the welfare of so many human beings is a matter of the smallest consideration, I am sure it can be only want of information at many

points, and misinformation on others that could induce you not to concur most fully in what I am at last determined to carry into effect. Your judgment has been most grossly abused in the representations which we know have been made to you. They are altogether unfounded in truth and therefore in the last degree cruel and insulting. I believe that you have been informed that Frederick said he would murder his Father. The words that Frederick made use of were these - 'We may thank God that we do not live in a barbarous Country, or we should have murdered each other before this.' George did everything to irritate Frederick a few days ago and though Frederick said nothing disrespectful (as I can produce respectable Witnesses to prove) he sent for the Constable (Mr. Baumber) and turned him out of doors. He remained with Mr. Baumber three days. He is now with my sister at Louth and is again taken into his father's favor who has allowed him a hundred pounds a year for the present and as soon as he sees what is resolved upon with respect to me he intends to go to London and study the law. George asserts that he had your authority for turning him out of doors. There is another and perhaps a stronger reason than any I have given for our separation, the impression which his conduct may produce upon the minds of his family not to mention the perpetual one of such degrading epithets to myself and children as a husband and a Father and above all a person of his sacred profession ought particularly to avoid. A short time since he had a large knife and loaded gun in his room. The latter he took into the kitchen to try before he went to bed. He was going to fire it off through the kitchen Window but was dissuaded. With the knife he said he would kill Frederick by stabbing him in the jugular vein and in the heart. I remonstrated with him on having such dangerous weapons and told him he would be killing himself. He said he should not do this but he would kill others and Frederick should be one. I do not say this to injure my poor husband in your opinion but only to convince you that in the state of mind in which he is at times it is not safe for his family to live with him. You cannot but understand Sir that when I express my sentiments on this subject more strongly than I am accustomed to do, nothing but the urgency of the case could have induced me so to do, and that I should be the last person in the world to act as a principal in an affair of this kind had it been possible for us to accommodate our differences in any other manner, having I think furnished a proof by submitting to the life I have led for more than twenty years that matrimonial obligations were in my eyes of far greater importance than mere personal considerations. But when insult is aggravated by Injury the burden of such accumulated ills is grievous and insufferable. I shall take lodgings at Louth as soon as possible. My brother bids me say he will come over with me to Tealby to converse with you on this unfortunate subject or will be happy to see you at his house whichever you may prefer.

    I remain, my dear Sir,
    Your affectionate daughter
    Eliza Tennyson

## Bayons Manor and Somersby

In 1806, by way of compensation for being disinherited, Tennyson's father was appointed Rector of Somersby and Bag Enderby, and in 1808 moved into Somersby Rectory. From that time on, the Tennyson family was divided between the spacious grandeur of Bayons and the crowded squalor of Somersby. Those at Bayons saw the Somersby 'brood' as reprehensible, while George looked at his more comfortably housed relatives with bitter sarcasm. 'We are three and twenty in family and sleep five or six in a room', he wrote to his brother, 'Truly we have great accommodation for Mrs Russell and her suite. We have not the house at Brighton nor the castle at Brancepeth. . . .'[12] By 1820, he and his wife were sharing the modest rectory with eleven children and, surprisingly, at least ten servants.

**52**
**Unknown artist**
Bayons Manor
1820
Photograph of drawing 26.5 x 37.5 cms
Lincolnshire County Council:
Tennyson Research Centre, Lincoln

**53**
**Unknown artist**
Bayons Manor
No date
Photograph of drawing 26.2 x 55 cms
Lincolnshire County Council:
Tennyson Research Centre, Lincoln

The self-styled ancestral home of the Tennysons, purchased by George Tennyson between 1783 and 1787, shown here before and after its reconstruction. Charles Tennyson D'Eyncourt's ambitious programme of building (which included a dining room to seat two hundred people) was a part of his dream of establishing a family dynasty at Bayons. Although he had considerable architectural talent, his efforts were ultimately unsuccessful, and ridiculed by the local aristocracy. Colonel Cracroft, after a visit to Bayons Manor, wrote in his diary:

Whoever would think for all the pomp and circumstance and pretended ancestry of Bayons Manor that its owner was the son of my grandfather's attorney at Market Rasen? Beautifully done in every respect as is Bayons its the ridicule of the county. . . . I was walking about it . . . its sham keep and drawbridge and moat, and thought what an exquisite piece of tomfoolery it is - but still an enchanting pretty situation.[13]

**54**
**Unknown artist**
Somersby Rectory
No date
Photograph 15 x 19 cms
Lincolnshire County Council:
Tennyson Research Centre, Lincoln

It is noticeable that Tennyson, his brothers and his sisters all looked back at their time at Somersby with affection. Even though the atmosphere of the house must at times have been intolerable, the mood was lightened by the Lincolnshire countryside, occasions which were undoubtedly convivial, and most of all by the writing and the reading of poetry.

**55**
**Alfred Lord Tennyson**
Description of Somersby
No date
Lincolnshire County Council:
Tennyson Research Centre, Lincoln

Somersby is a village situated under a chalk-hill called in the dialogue of this county, a wold - a village shadowed by tall elm trees, with here & there a sand-rock falling out of the soil: two brooks meet at the bottom of the glebe field.

**56**
**Alfred Lord Tennyson**
Notes recorded by Hallam Tennyson
No date
Lincolnshire County Council:
Tennyson Research Centre, Lincoln

A friend of the Somersby days writes:
You have seen a sketch of the house where he was born and if you had known it as I knew it you would have a loving recollection of the sweet woodbine which peeped into the bay window of the nursery, of the vaulted dining-room with its stained glass in the arched windows making 'butterfly's souls' as his brother Charles called them about the room, of the beautiful stone chimney-piece carved by their father, of the pleasant drawing-room furnished with bookshelves & yellow curtains sofa & chair, which looked out in the pleasant lawn overshadowed on one side by a Whych-elm walk and on the other by a fine larch tree and a sycamore; flat for a space and then sloping down to a field at whose foot ran the brook the charm and beauty of which haunted him through life.

You would have delighted to recall the wooded hollow of Holywell, its old spring, its sandstone rocks, its flowers and mosses and ferns. You will have looked long ago for the name of Byron which he carved on the day he heard of Byron's death, a day when the whole world seemed darkened to him, he said.

**57**
**[Arthur Tennyson (1814-99)]**
Gate into Holywell wood
No date
Pen and ink 13 x 9 cms
Lincolnshire County Council:
Tennyson Research Centre, Lincoln

A wood near Somersby. Here Tennyson saw his future wife, Emily Sellwood, greeting her with the words, which she never forgot: 'Are you a Dryad or an Oread wandering here?' According to Hallam Tennyson 'He delighted too to recall the rare richness of the bowery lanes: the ancient Norman cross standing in the churchyard, close to the door of the quaint little church: the wooded hollow of Holywell: the cold springs flowing from under the sandstone rocks: the flowers, the mosses, and the ferns.'[14]

## Poetry

**58**
**Alfred Lord Tennyson & Charles Tennyson**
*Poems, by Two Brothers*
London: W. Simpkin and R. Marshall; Louth: J. and J. Jackson, 1827
Lincolnshire County Council:
Tennyson Research Centre, Lincoln

Tennyson shared the authorship of this, his first publication, with his elder brothers Frederick and Charles. Charles in particular had many of his younger brother's poetic gifts. In 1830 he published a volume of sonnets that was praised by both Samuel Taylor Coleridge and William Wordsworth. The latter wrote to W.R. Hamilton that same year: 'We have a respectable show of blossom in poetry. Two brothers of the name of Tennyson, in particular, are not a little promising'. Indeed, according to Thomas Cooper, Wordsworth 'had thought an elder brother of Tennyson at first the better poet'[15]. His life was shadowed by a serious opium addiction but, as Vicar of Grasby, he was an admired and respected figure.

Inscribed on front endpaper: 'The two brothers were Alfred Tennyson (Poet Laureate) and his brother Charles; their first attempts at poetry, these poems were printed in Louth, and sold to various friends amongst others my grandfather George [W] Maddison and his wife Frances Elizabeth F.A.T. Maddison'

Always acutely self-critical of his works, Tennyson later described the volume as 'early rot'.

Cat. 59

**59**
**Charles Tennyson Turner (1808-79)**
Portrait by J.E. Mayall
*c.*1864
Photograph 25.5 x 20.5 cms
Lincolnshire County Council:
Tennyson Research Centre, Lincoln

**60**
**Arthur Tennyson**
[Self portrait]
No date
Pencil 14.7 x 10.5 cms
Lincolnshire County Council:
Tennyson Research Centre, Lincoln

Arthur Tennyson was a talented artist who suffered, like most of the family, from a highly nervous temperament. His drawings, usually of devils and male grotesques, do however have a rough kind of humour, a quality that is not entirely absent from some of Tennyson's best poetry. Fitzgerald said of 'St. Simeon Stylites', 'This is one of the Poems A.T. would read with grotesque Grimness, especially at such passages as "Coughs, Aches, Stitches, etc."'[16]

**61**

**Alfred Lord Tennyson**

Portrait by Arthur Tennyson

No date

Pencil with some inking over 16 x 8 cms

Lincolnshire County Council:

Tennyson Research Centre, Lincoln

A caricature of Tennyson, with the caption 'Top of his profession'.

**62**

**Arthur Tennyson**

*Brothers in misery*

No date

Pen and ink, pencil 19.5 x 24 cms

Lincolnshire County Council:

Tennyson Research Centre, Lincoln

Arthur Tennyson's sketch of Alfred (left) and Charles (right), with its humorous caption, compares interestingly with the more serious tone of Tennyson's later recollections of his childhood misery.

**63**

**Alfred Lord Tennyson**

Conversations recorded by Hallam Tennyson

No date

Lincolnshire County Council:

Tennyson Research Centre, Lincoln

In my youth I knew much greater unhappiness than I have known in later life. When I was about twenty, I used to feel moods of misery unutterable! I remember once in London the realization *coming* over me, of the *whole* of its inhabitants lying horizontal a few hundred years hence.

The smallness and emptiness of life sometimes overwhelmed me -. I used to experience sensations of a state almost impossible to describe in words; it was not exactly a trance but the world seemed dead around - and myself only alive.

It might have been the state - described by Sᵗ Paul "Whether in the body I cannot tell; or whether out of the body I cannot tell." It sometimes came upon me after repeating my name to myself; through excess of realising my own personality I seem to get outside of myself.

**64**

**Alfred Lord Tennyson**

Biographical notes referring to his early life

No date

Lincolnshire County Council:

Tennyson Research Centre, Lincoln

The notes are brief and corrective. It was in poetry, and especially in *Maud*, that Tennyson would face his early childhood experiences.

Poems by Two Brothers. The preface states, written from 15 to 18.

I was 17 Charles was 18. The publisher dated the book in the year following the publication.

You follow'd a blind guide in Tennyson land. The Moated Grange is an imaginary house in the fen. I never so much as dreamed of Baumber's farm as the abode of Mariana & the character of Baumber was so ludicrously unlike that of the Northern Farmer that it really makes me wonder how anyone can invent such untruths.

The cottage to which I sometimes resorted at Mablethorpe was close under the sea bank & does not seem to be the one portrayed in Tiresias.

The British Quarterly is wrong. I never heard Spedding make a speech at the Union.

My mother never lived in Westgate Terrace. I lodged with my grandmother & aunt.

The notes are good but once or twice wrong.

eg "Cut prejudice": your own prejudice. No, those of others for it is added. Do it gently.

My Schwärmerei for Byron entirely ceased when I was about 18 & I dont think I have ever opened him since.

Cat. 62

# 4. School and University

## Early education

In 1816, after a solid grounding in the classics from his tutors and his father, Tennyson joined his elder brothers Frederick and Charles at Louth Grammar School. Despite the kindness of his mother's sister, Mary Anne Fytche, he was not happy, and after three years he returned home to be again educated by his father. The family home thus became a place of learning. His father's tuition was classical and thorough, if rather unpredictable, and he was quick to encourage his son's poetic talent: 'My father who was a sort of Poet himself thought so highly of my first essay that he prophesied I should be the greatest Poet of the Time.' He also offered some constructive criticism: 'My father once said to me, "Don't write so rhythmically, break your lines occasionally for the sake of variety."'[17]

### 65
**T.W. Wallis**
Louth Market Place
c.1848
Print from stone engraving 23.6 x 38.8 cms
Lincolnshire County Council:
Tennyson Research Centre, Lincoln

Tennyson was at Louth Grammar School for three years. He hated the school so much that in later years he refused to walk down the street where it stood.

In the centre of the picture is Jackson's printing house, which produced Tennyson's first publication, *Poems By Two Brothers* (1827).

### 66
**George Clayton Tennyson**
Commonplace Book
1807
Lincolnshire County Council:
Tennyson Research Centre, Lincoln

The contents of George Clayton Tennyson's commonplace book are at once wide-ranging and intricate, showing the extent of George Clayton Tennyson's learning, and his evident qualifications as a tutor to Tennyson. Entries range from a treatise on book-binding to biographical lists of Italian artists. It also contains some examples of his poetry. The poem *The Wandering Jew* gives something of the flavour of his writing. These are the opening lines:

O Stranger, why enquire the hapless fate
Of one most sorely scath'd by power supreme

My guilt passed utterance why should I relate
All tale of Woe will bid thine eyes to stream
With pity's kindly drops - my fortunes teem
With incident so horrible and rare
That thou incredulous perchance mayst deem
Reasons divested of her throne and care
And age to have installed the second childhood there

### 67
**Pindar**
*Pindari Carmina*
London: T. Cadell and W. Davies, 1814
Lincolnshire County Council:
Tennyson Research Centre, Lincoln

### 68
**Horace**
*Works*
London: G and W.B. Whittaker, 1822
Lincolnshire County Council:
Tennyson Research Centre, Lincoln

A Greek, Latin, Hebrew and Syriac scholar of some distinction, George Clayton Tennyson had a library quite capable of educating his sons in the classics. 'My father said that he himself received a good but not a regular classical education', writes Hallam Tennyson in the *Memoir*, 'At any rate he became an accurate scholar, the author thoroughly drummed into him being Horace; whom he disliked in proportion. He would lament, "They use *me* as a lesson-book at school, and they will call me "that horrible Tennyson." It was not till many years after boyhood that I could like Horace. Byron expressed what I felt, "Then farewell Horace whom I hated so." Indeed I was so overdosed with Horace that I hardly do him justice even now that I am old."[18]

## Cambridge

In 1827, he entered Trinity College, Cambridge, and for the first time became closely acquainted with people outside his immediate family. His greatest friend was undoubtedly Arthur Hallam, who died of apoplexy aged only 22. Tennyson's great poem *In Memoriam*, seventeen years in the making, is dedicated to him.

### 69
**James Spedding (1808-1881)**
Self portrait
No date
Pencil, white and red chalk 37 x 26 cms
Spedding Collection

James Spedding was, after Hallam, Tennyson's closest friend at Cambridge. 'He was the Pope among us young men', Tennyson later remarked, 'the wisest man I know'[19].   When, in 1832, Spedding's younger brother Edward died, Tennyson wrote the first of his great elegies, 'To J.S.'. 'The lines to J.S. are perfect', Hallam wrote to Tennyson in October 1832, 'James, I am sure, will be most grateful'. The poem began before Edward's death, and the opening lines had been sent to Edward by James who had been enquiring about Tennyson's *Ode*. Probably Tennyson's first thought was to write an ode on the death of his father, who is the other figure mourned within the poem.

### To J.S.

The wind, that beats the mountain, blows
More softly round the open wold,
And gently comes the world to those
That are cast in gentle mould.

And me this knowledge bolder made,
Or else I had not dared to flow
In these words toward you, and invade
Even with a verse your holy woe.

'Tis strange that those we lean on most,
Those in whose laps our limbs are nursed,
Fall into shadow, soonest lost:
Those we love first are taken first.

God gives us love. Something to love
He lends us; but, when love is grown
To ripeness, that on which it throve
Falls off, and love is left alone.

This is the curse of time. Alas!
In grief I am not all unlearned;
Once through mine own doors Death did pass;
One went, who never hath returned.

He will not smile-not speak to me
Once more. Two years his chair is seen
Empty before us. That was he
Without whose life I had not been.

Your loss is rarer; for this star
Rose with you through a little arc
Of heaven, nor having wandered far
Shot on the sudden into dark.

I knew your brother: his mute dust
I honour and his living worth:
A man more pure and bold and just
Was never born into the earth.

I have not looked upon you nigh,
Since that dear soul hath fallen asleep.
Great Nature is more wise than I:
I will not tell you not to weep.

And though mine own eyes fill with dew,
Drawn from the spirit through the brain,
I will not even preach to you,
'Weep, weeping dulls the inward pain.'

Let Grief be her own mistress still.
She loveth her own anguish deep
More than much pleasure. Let her will
Be done-to weep or not to weep.

I will not say, 'God's ordinance
Of Death is blown in every wind;'
For that is not a common chance
That takes away a noble mind.

His memory long will live alone
In all our hearts, as mournful light
That broods above the fallen sun,
And dwells in heaven half the night.

Vain solace! Memory standing near
Cast down her eyes, and in her throat
Her voice seemed distant, and a tear
Dropt on the letters as I wrote.

I wrote I know not what. In truth,
How *should I* soothe you anyway,
Who miss the brother of your youth?
Yet something I did wish to say:

For he too was a friend to me:
Both are my friends, and my true breast
Bleedeth for both; yet it may be
That only silence suiteth best.

Words weaker than your grief would make
Grief more. 'Twere better I should cease
Although myself could almost take
The place of him that sleeps in peace.

Sleep sweetly, tender heart, in peace:
Sleep, holy spirit, blessed soul,
While the stars burn, the moons increase,
And the great ages onward roll.

Sleep till the end, true soul and sweet.
Nothing comes to thee new or strange.
Sleep full of rest from head to feet;
Lie still, dry dust, secure of change.

70
### Edward Spedding (1811-1832)
Portrait by James Spedding
Pencil 18.2 x 13.3 cms
Spedding Collection

Edward Spedding was a friend of Arthur Hallam, but had certain suspicions about Hallam's real seriousness. Edward attacked Hallam on 16 August 1831 in his letter to his brother James:

To me our admirable friend seems to have written his article [in the *Englishman's Magazine*, 1831] in language which to most of his readers will give a glossary far more than the Canterbury Tales with their peculiar misfortune that whereas the words themselves are familiar, this combination of them into forms as unusual to ninety-nine readers out of a hundred, makes them seem what you and I know they are not, phrases without thoughts. Moreover I quarrel with the flippancy sprinkled throughout the Article, which seems to me to have been condescended to in the same spirit which made him write that unfortunate poem about the North Pole.

Cat. 69

Cat. 70

James resisted this condemnation of Hallam: on 7 September 1831 he wrote

I do not agree with you as to A.H.H's flippancy. It seems to me to be all very graceful & Courteous - and the medium nicely hit. But we always differ on this subject, as on most others.

James even suggested that Edward is simply prejudiced against Hallam:

I like to be amused with him & his pursuits & his amusements - you, if I mistake not, despise him so cordially that even where his taste coincides with your own natural taste you will not laugh or weep with him - if you fancy that a thing would please him it is enough to make it displease you. But that is my present opinion of your temper in this matter - of course you do not believe it to be true.

It is clear from Hallam's letters to Edward Spedding that Edward took his criticisms direct to the offending author. Hallam admits to a certain abstruseness:

It is true I thought more of myself and the Truth, as I thought I perceived it, than of my probable readers. This, you will say, was selfish, because I ought to have done whatever would do most good to Alfred.

He admits he wrote:

in a Magazine humour, and the result was trash that you are very probably ashamed of, and so am I. I am inclined however to think that both you & your brother something overrate the abstruseness of my writing . . .

In all the exchanges there is a prickly self-respect on both sides. Throughout the circle around Tennyson there were high expectations, a constant analysis and judgment of one another, and from it all a stimulus to achievement. When Edward died, Hallam wrote to Tennyson:

Emily has probably told you of the death of Edward Spedding, cut off in the prime of life & the freshness of ardent feelings. He was more sensitive than his brother, but tempered that susceptibility with something of James' calmness.

71
**Alfred Lord Tennyson**
Portrait attributed to James Spedding
*c.*1831
Pencil 19.7 x 14 cms
By Courtesy of The National Portrait Gallery, London

Spedding was a talented artist, and his informal portraits provide an invaluable record of Tennyson and his circle.

## Prizes

Neither Hallam, Spedding or Tennyson achieved conventional academic distinction whilst at Cambridge, but each excelled in their own individual ways. Spedding and Hallam won the college oration prize in successive years, and Tennyson was awarded the Chancellor's Gold Medal for his poem *Timbuctoo*.

### 72
**The Oration Prize**
1830
Silver H 28 cms
Spedding Collection

James Spedding was the first to win the oration prize cup (the legacy of Dr Hooper) on Commemoration Day on the 16th of December 1830. The candidates for the 1831 prize, as it happened, were called upon to give their orations at the same event and Hallam was among them. On receiving the cup James Spedding sent it to his home at Mirehouse and wrote to his mother:

I have not only received the accompanying cup: but likewise the various complements of all sorts & sizes: and not only received complements, but likewise held communion with the Poet Laureate . . . have likewise been introduced to the master of Trinity and the brother of the Master of Trinity: not only been introduced to him but likewise talked to him, even with the great poet -& heard him dilate largely on matters moral, poetical, and philosophical - also received a free offer to walk with him and talk with him, which if the Gods permit, I mean to avail myself of.

Thus Wordsworth and Southey were both present as Spedding and Hallam performed.

### 73
**James Spedding**
*Apology for the Moral and Literary Character of the Nineteenth Century*
Cambridge, 1830
Spedding Collection

The text of Spedding's prize oration. It begins:

That every man who comes into the world has a twofold duty to perform, - the duty of living well himself, and the duty of persuading other men by his example and instruction to live well also, - is a truth which few can be so hardy as to dispute, or so dull as not to feel. Neither is it too much to assume that, as no man ought to reprove another unless to make him better, so he must be very careful that the reproof be both temperate and fully called for; inasmuch as an undue rebuke is worse than an approval.

### 74
**The Oration Prize**
1831
Silver H 36 cms
Lady Elton Collection

Hallam won the oration prize the year after James Spedding. His oration was on the subject of History, and his argument was that the independent party of Oliver Cromwell had been justified 'in ceasing the Government and putting force on a legislative body, in the year 1648'[20]. Robert Monteith wrote to Monckton Milnes, 10 February 1831: 'Hallam in all likelihood is to have the declamation prize this year; - it was verily splendid to see the poet Wordsworth's face, for he was there, kindle as H. proceeded with it'[21].

### 75
**Chancellor's gold medal**
T. Wyon
1829
Lincolnshire County Council:
Tennyson Research Centre, Lincoln

Prize medal awarded to Tennyson in 1829 for his poem 'Timbuctoo', the first poem written in blank verse to win the prize. Charles Wordsworth, son of Christopher Wordsworth Master of Trinity and younger brother of the poet, commented: 'It is certainly a wonderful production; and if it had come out with Lord Byron's name, it would have been thought as fine as anything he wrote'[22]. He also commented that 'Spedding and Hallam delivered their prize orations in this chapel. Tennyson, likewise, should have read the prize poem himself in the senate house; he blamed shyness for his failure to do so'. Hallam also contributed a poem on the same subject, in terza rima, and it was through the contest that he and Tennyson became acquainted.

### 76
**Various authors**
*Prolusiones Academicae*
Cambridge: 1829
Lincolnshire County Council:
Tennyson Research Centre, Lincoln

Contains the first publication of *Timbuctoo*. When the poem came up for republication several years later Tennyson, who had refused permission for other reprintings, wrote: 'I could have wished that poor *Timbuctoo* might have been suffered to slide quietly off, with all its errors, into forgetfulness.'

**77**
**J. Bluck** after **F. Mackenzie**
Chapel of Trinity College
1814
Aquatint 26 x 19.5 cms
Spedding Collection

Spedding and Hallam delivered their prize orations in this chapel. Tennyson, likewise, should have read his prize poem himself, but in the Senate House.

## Cambridge Contemporaries and The Apostles

In 1829 Tennyson became a member of the informal but exclusive club, the Cambridge Conversazione Society, better known as the Cambridge Apostles. This was considered to be a high achievement, for the members were traditionally (by their own reckoning, at least) the most brilliant members of Trinity College.

Tennyson resigned after shyness prevented him from reading a paper entitled *Ghosts*. He had been in the society for only three months, but its witty and intellectual atmosphere, so stimulating after the seclusion of home life, was to provide him with lasting friendships. Hallam, Spedding, Monkton Milnes, W.H. Thompson and Trench were all fellow Apostles, and became intimate friends.

**78**
**Frederick Denison Maurice (1805-1872)**
Portrait by Lowes Dickinson
1859
Pastel 48.4 x 36.6 cms
Trinity College, Cambridge

It was Maurice, with John Sterling, who established the serious moral tone of the society. He left Cambridge the year Tennyson arrived, but the two men became close friends, Maurice becoming godfather to Tennyson's eldest son, Hallam.

**79**
**Richard Chenevix Trench (1807-1886)**
Portrait by Samuel Laurence
Watercolour 47.4 x 34.3 cms
Spedding Collection

**80**
**Richard Chenevix Trench**
Portrait after photograph by John Watkins
Engraving by D.J. Pound 30.2 x 19.1 cms
Trinity College, Cambridge

**81**
**Richard Chenevix Trench**
Portrait by unknown artist
1836
Lithograph 36.3 x 29.4 cms
Trinity College, Cambridge

Trench (who later became Archbishop of Dublin) was a friend of Tennyson, but he was opposed to what he saw as the harmful self-indulgence of his character. After *Poems, Chiefly Lyrical* appeared in 1830, he wrote to W.B. Donne that Tennyson's 'friends at Cambridge will materially injure him if he does not beware - no young man under any circumstances should believe that he *has* done anything, but still be forward looking'[23]. Tennyson's poem *The Palace of Art* was in turn a challenge to Trench's remark, 'Tennyson, we cannot live in art.' It is prefaced with an introduction addressed to Trench:

I send you here a sort of allegory,
(For you will understand it) of a soul,
A sinful soul possessed of many gifts,
A spacious garden full of flowering weeds,
A glorious Devil, large in heart and brain,
That did love Beauty only, (Beauty seen
In all varieties of mould and mind)
And Knowledge for its beauty, seeing not
That Beauty, Good, and Knowledge, are three sisters
That doat upon each other, friends to man,
Living together under the same roof,
And never can be sundered without tears.
And he that shuts Love out, in turn shall be
Shut out from Love, and on her threshold lie
Howling in outer darkness. Not for this
Was common clay ta'en from the common earth
Moulded by God, and tempered with the tears
Of angels to the perfect shape of man.

Tennyson felt he had no need to be warned of the seductions and dangers of living only in art; nevertheless, he deals with the theme brilliantly in *The Lady of Shalott*, showing that those who live a half life are indeed doomed.

**82**
**Richard Monckton Milnes (1809-1885)**
Portrait by Caroline Smith
No date
Pencil and watercolour 21.5 x 17.5 cms
Spedding Collection

**83**
**Richard Monckton Milnes**
Portrait after George Richmond
No date
Engraving by William Holl 47.6 x 37.7 cms
Trinity College, Cambridge

Cat. 71

Monkton Milnes, later Lord Houghton, was elected an Apostle in 1830, the same day as Tennyson. J.W. Blakesley reported this double event to Trench:

Milnes is now an Apostle. The Society doth not, I think, gain much from him, but he will leave Cambridge in a few weeks. . . . The Society has received a great addition in Hallam and in Alfred Tennyson. . . Truly one of the mighty of the earth. You will be delighted with him when you see him.'[24]

Milnes and Tennyson were always on friendly terms, and Tennyson asked Milnes to attend him when receiving the peerage, but their temperaments were very different. Milnes's easy wit and wide acquaintance, which earned him the nickname "The Bird of Paradox", contrasted strongly with the seriousness of Tennyson's character.

## 84

### William Henry Brookfield (1809-1874)
Portrait after Samuel Laurence
No date
Lithograph by J.H. Lynch 43.1 x 30.3 cms
Trinity College, Cambridge

Brookfield was President of the Cambridge Union and was, reputedly, one of the wittiest men of his generation. He was ordained to the curacy of Maltby in 1834, and in 1841 married Julia Elton, a cousin of Arthur Hallam. After his death in 1874, Tennyson wrote the following sonnet:

**To the Rev. W.H. Brookfield**

Brooks, for they called you so that knew you best,
Old Brooks, who loved so well to mouth my rhymes,
How oft we two have heard St Mary's chimes!
How oft the Cantab supper, host and guest,
Would echo helpless laughter to your jest!
How oft with him we paced that walk of limes,
Him, the lost light of those dawn-golden times,
Who loved you well! Now both are gone to rest.
You man of humorous-melancholy mark,
Dead of some inward agony - is it so?
Our kindlier, trustier Jaques, past away!
I cannot laud this life, it looks so dark:
*Ekias onar* - dream of a shadow, go -
God bless you. I shall join you in a day.

## 85

### William Hepworth Thompson (1810-1886)
Portrait by unknown artist
No date
Pencil 17.9 x 12.8 cms
Spedding Collection

Thompson, later Master of Trinity College, was never in any doubt as to Tennyson's poetic genius. On seeing him first enter the Hall at Trinity, he said, 'That man must be a poet', and in later life,

when asked by Montague Butler '*At the time*, did you consider [Hallam] or Tennyson the greater man?' replied at once, 'Oh Tennyson, without a doubt'[25].

## 86

### William Makepeace Thackeray (1811-1863)
Portrait by Samuel Laurence
c.1852
Pastel 43.2 x 35.4 cms
Spedding Collection

Thackeray was an undergraduate at Trinity with Tennyson, but was not asked to become an Apostle; the two got to know each other later in life. Such was the prestige of the Apostles, according to Thackeray, that it was considered to set a man apart to be seen with William Brookfield, who was not an Apostle himself, but who was friendly with several.

Thackeray later described Tennyson as having 'the cachet of a great man. His conversation is often delightful, I think, full of breadth manliness and humour: he reads all sorts of things, swallows them and digests them like a great poetical boa-constrictor as he is. . . . Perhaps it is his great big yellow face and growling voice that has had an impression on me.'[26]

## 87

### James Spedding
Tennyson and a group of Apostles
No date
Pencil 32.5 x 23.4 cms
Spedding Collection

Despite the seriousness of the Apostles, humour was never far away. Robert Martin tells us that Tennyson's party piece, illustrated here, was to imitate the rising sun. As the sun emerged from the clouds he would gradually open his eyes and mouth, then slowly close them up as the sun returned to obscurity.[27]

The figures are not easily identifiable, but the figure which appears upside-down could be another drawing of Arthur Hallam.

# 5. Arthur Hallam

Cat. 96

Arthur Hallam (1811-33) was the most important figure in the early lives of two great men. William Gladstone, the future Prime Minister, described their time together at Eton as 'the zenith of my boyhood', and Tennyson benefitted immeasurably both from his society and from the instinctive sympathy he showed for his poetry. Hallam's affection was in part for Tennyson, but also for the poet's sister Emily. Much against the wishes of his father, Henry Hallam the great Whig historian, Hallam and Emily became engaged.

In life, the force and brilliance of Hallam's personality created an indelible impression on those who knew him, but it was in death that he seemed to cast a spell over his contemporaries. 'When shall I see his like?', wrote Gladstone. For Tennyson he seemed, simply, 'as near perfection as a mortal man can be', but a more subtle change took place: the trusted friend became the poet's insistent muse.

88
**Arthur Henry Hallam (1811-1833)**
Portrait by Sir Martin Arthur Shee
*c.*1830
Oil on canvas
76.2 x 63.5 cms
Eton College

Hallam's leaving portrait from Eton, where he was considered the most brilliant classical scholar of his day.

89
**Eton Lists 1822-25**
Eton: E. Williams 1827
Eton College

Hallam's name appears alongside that of William Gladstone, the future Prime Minister and his closest friend at Eton.

90
[W.E. Gladstone]
**The Eton Miscellany**
Eton: T. Ingalton 1827
Eton College

Gladstone, already politically-minded, includes a poem in praise of the politician George Canning, who was pleased with it when it was shown to him.

91
Various authors
**Musae Etonensis**
1820-9
Eton College

92
**William Ewart Gladstone (1809-1898)**
Portrait from a copy by F.H. Bradley
1841
Oil on canvas 152.4 x 121.9 cms
Eton College

Gladstone had a long-lasting, but never easy, friendship with Tennyson. He disapproved of the morbid sentiments of *Locksley Hall Sixty Years After*, while Tennyson disapproved of Gladstone's liberal policy towards Ireland ('I love Mr Gladstone but I hate his present Irish policy' he wrote to the *Times* on 28 June 1892). Nevertheless they had considerable mutual respect for each other. Gladstone wrote in the press: 'The state of contemporary judgement on the whole does not leave any doubt that for this period of history Lord Tennyson heads the band of the Immortals. . . . Probably no English poet, except it be Wordsworth, has paid so intense and absorbing a devotion to his muse.' On top of this, the memory of Hallam was a constant reminder of what they had in common. Gladstone's comment on this friendship might have come from Tennyson: 'He had in one point a large advantage over me. He had evidently, from the first, a large share of cultivated domestic education. With a father occupied in diversified business, I had none.'[28]

**93**

**Alfred Lord Tennyson**
Draft letter to William Ewart Gladstone
14 July 1880
Lincolnshire County Council:
Tennyson Research Centre, Lincoln

My dear Gladstone

Our common friend, Mrs Brookfield not venturing to address you except thro' me has somewhat strangely I think sent me this petitionary letter to be forwarded to you . . . Now I know you once told me that a literary name had no political influence - nevertheless - if but in consideration of our friendship, I trust that you will regard her claim not unfavourably and believe me Yours ever A Tennyson

**94**

**William Ewart Gladstone**
Letter to Alfred Lord Tennyson
16 July 1880
Lincolnshire County Council:
Tennyson Research Centre, Lincoln

My dear Tennyson

I have just received your letter and I write at once to say that I will make the necessary enquiries and do the best I can though I fear it cannot be much
Ever yours sincerely
W E Gladstone

**95**

**Arthur Henry Hallam**
Portrait by James Spedding
*c.*1831
Photograph of drawing 9.8 x 7.6 cms
Trinity College, Cambridge

The portrait, showing Hallam in profile, can be compared with the bust of Hallam now at Trinity College, Cambridge.

**96**

**Arthur Henry Hallam**
Portrait by James Spedding
*c.*1828
Pencil 22.4 x 17.2 cms
Spedding Collection

**97**

**Arthur Henry Hallam**
Portrait by James Spedding
*c.*1828
Pencil 27 x 16.6 cms
Spedding Collection

Spedding's drawings are of a more mature Hallam than the slightly plump, almost cherubic face in the Eton portrait. He is shown as physically frail, but with a touch of the dandy, and this is in keeping with a figure who was personally attractive, but who at the same time experienced, according to his father, 'a considerable depression of spirits which had been painfully observed at times by those who watched him most, from the time of his leaving Eton, and even before'.

**98**

**Arthur Henry Hallam**
Letter to Alfred Lord Tennyson
1831
Lincolnshire County Council:
Tennyson Research Centre, Lincoln

My dear Alfred

Will you tell Charles that Term begins on the 14th. April. I wish very much to hear from you at some length, and intended to have tempted you to write by writing myself a long letter: but I have not time at this moment. I am going to London tomorrow, girded up for warfare. I hope to fight like a true knight, although Emily's eyes will not be there to "rain influence". Oret pro nobis. I shall write to her in a few days, and will send at the same time Leigh Hunt's review of you & Charles, and a very contemptible Poem of my own, in which I have bartered the immortal part of me to a Darwinian demon for a barren chance of being in the Calendar. Fare thee well. I hope you do fare well, and make head against "despondency and madness". Distribute my love about & believe me

Yours for ever,
*A H Hallam*

**99**

**Henry Hallam (1777-1859)**
Portrait by unknown artist
No date
Bronze medal D 6.3 cms
Spedding Collection

**100**

**Henry Hallam**
Portrait by unknown artist
No date
Bronze medal D 6.3 cms
Lady Elton Collection

Henry Hallam had been opposed to his son's marrying into the Tennyson family, which he saw as disrespectable, but the onset of old age and the early deaths of all but one of his children mellowed his opinions to the extent that he became almost a surrogate father to Emily Tennyson. He made provision for her, and for Tennyson in his will.

**101**

**Ellen Hallam (1816-37)**
Portrait by unknown artist
No date
Oil 8 x 6.5 cms
Lady Elton Collection

**102**

**Ellen Hallam**
Diary
1 November 1833 to 1 July 1834
Lady Elton Collection

The diary of Ellen Hallam, Arthur Hallam's sister, shows how Emily Tennyson, and to a lesser extent Tennyson himself, became very close to the Hallam family after Arthur Hallam's death:

Jan. 9th Thursday
An agitating, distressing day.
Mamma - received a letter from Mrs Tennyson. Poor Emily seems in a wretched state of health like a frail, delicate flower she sank beneath the violence of storm. I shudder when I think of what her sufferings must be - the finest earthly object of *such* a creature -! Oh! Emily, dear, Emily, how I wished I could mourn with thee -! The society of *his* sister would not but be pleasing to thee, &, talking of him we should find sweetness in grief. But thou art *far, far away.* Thou wilt *never* see these lines, & in all human probability the agonising joy of embracing each other on earth will be denied us. But we have no right to repine what have we deserved at the hands of God, that such bliss should be ours? Perhaps such a meeting would be more productive of pain than pleasure - at any rate, what God wills is best. But oh! thou dear sufferer when I think of the heartaches for thee. . .

Cat. 103

**103**

**Emily Jesse, née Tennyson (1811-1889)**
Portrait by unknown artist
No date
Photograph
H 8.5 cms
Lincolnshire County Council:
Tennyson Research Centre, Lincoln

**104**

**Arthur Henry Hallam**
Letter to Emily Tennyson
12 December 1832
Lincolnshire County Council:
Tennyson Research Centre, Lincoln

My dearest Emily

I am much grieved to think what your grief must be in leaving Somersby. I hardly dare endeavor to console you, but I trust you feel the necessity of summoning up all the powers of your mind to meet the event with composure & patience, if not with fortitude. Surely it must be some relief to you that you go not to a distant place, but to Dalby, the *second home* of your childhood, a spot endeared by numberless early associations, & having the same neighbourhood as Somersby itself. This must comfort you, I think; and since you must indeed go to Dalby, it is well that you should keep it much before your mind, as I doubt not you do. Yet - shall I own it, Emily? I could bring myself to with it were not so, and that when you left your home you had left altogether the country. There is a hunger of imagination praying upon your mind which I want to see blunted by a complete, or at least considerable change of circumstances. Do you think me cruel for saying this? I speak only in what I think your real & permanent interest. To secure your welfare I would assent to anything & everything - even to the temporary wounding of your feelings. I too love Somersby. How dearly! But I love it *principally* for your sake. I trust I am not too late to see it once more, to take a farewell of it with you - a last farewell of objects & places eternally engraven on my heart, because connected with a passion that has made the destiny of my life. I will not sadden myself more by writing more about it.

Tell me - you do not surely leave Somersby before Xmas? I purpose being with you the *twenty third*; Sunday I believe. I would fain have come before the *twentieth*, for that day is to me a saint's day - can you guess why, or does your perplexingly short memory leave you at fault? But my father particularly wishes me to dine on the 21st. with Mr Justice Bosanquet who has made me a very kind offer lately connected with the law. Will your aunt be in town at that time? I much wish to see her. I hope her being in town henceforward may be made advantageous to us. You never answered a question I once asked you about the precise tenor of a certain speech made by her to Fred; however I shall soon be in a condition to ascertain for myself. Has anything been heard lately of the old man? What does he think of your change to Dalby? I fear you are rather more in his way there: but we may defy him; we have done with him; having refused to assist us when civilly asked, he has no longer the slightest influence on our conduct. We can despise his vices, and afford to pity him. Your reputable uncle, I see, is returned by a large majority for Lambeth. I wish the electors joy of him.

Alfred's book is prettily got up; there are, I believe, no errors except here & there in the stopping, [which] the reader's eye easily connects. The heaviest [source of] errors alas! consists of Alfred's own alterations. I hear the most rueful complaints from Cambridge of what he has done to the Lotuseaters Palace &c. However the men of Cambridge have bought *seventy-five* copies; a fact infinitely to their credit. There is a savage and stupid attack on poor Nal in the Literary Gazette - with such a parody on the Lady of Shalott! Poor Nal will die of it. But nobody minds the Lit. Gazette. Farewell, love; one letter more and *then*. Oh gioia! Oh ineffabile allegrezza!

Ever thy most affect:te
*Arthur.*

**105**

**Arthur Henry Hallam**

Poems in the hand of Emily Tennyson

Dated 18 February 1836

Notebook

Lincolnshire County Council:

Tennyson Research Centre, Lincoln

**106**

**Arthur Henry Hallam**

*Poems*

Lincolnshire County Council:

Tennyson Research Centre, Lincoln

The volume contains a sonnet, dated May 1829, in which Hallam describes the expansion of his friendship to include Tennyson as well as Gladstone:

To A.T.

Oh last in time, but worthy to be first
Of friends in rank, had not the father of good,
On my early spring one early gem bestowed,
A friend, with whom to share the best, and worst.
Him will I shut close to my heart for aye.
There's not a fibre quivers there, but is
His own, his heritage for woe, or bliss.
Thou would'st not have me such a charge betray.
Surely, if I be knit in brotherhood
So tender to that chief of all my love,
With thee I shall not loyalty eschew.
And well I ween not time, with ill, or good,
Shall thine affection e'er from mine remove,
Thou yearner for all fair things, and all true.

**107**

**Arthur Henry Hallam**

*To Alfred Tennyson*

No date

Holograph manuscript

Lincolnshire County Council:

Tennyson Research Centre, Lincoln

Those gothic windows are before me now,
Which long have shone dimlighted in my mind:
That slope of softest green, the brook below,
Old musty stalls, and tedded hay behind -
All have I seen; and simple tho' they be,
A mighty awe steals with them on my heart,
For they have grown and lasted as a part
Of thy dear self, up building thine and thee.
From yon tall fir, weathering the April rain
Came influence rare, that deepened into song,
Beauty looked for thee in the long grey field,
By Tufted knolls a [?] made thee strong:
Hence are the weapons, which thy spirit wields,
Musical thoughts of unexampled strain.

A.H.H.

**108**

**Alfred Lord Tennyson**

*Poems, Chiefly Lyrical*

London: Effingham Wilson, 1830

Lincolnshire County Council:

Tennyson Research Centre, Lincoln

The volume was originally to have been a joint publication with poems by Tennyson and Hallam, but Hallam withdrew following objections from his father. Tennyson later said of Hallam, 'He would have been known, if he had lived, as a great man but not as a great poet'[29], and it was his in tireless promotion of the volume and his efforts to see it succeed that he showed his real worth as a literary collaborator. His essay 'On Some of the Characteristics of Modern Poetry, and on the Lyrical Poems of Alfred Tennyson' was praised by W.B. Yeats as 'criticism which is of the best and rarest sort. If one set aside Shelley's essay on poetry and Browning's essay on Shelley, one does not know where to turn in modern English criticism for anything so philosophic - anything so fundamental and radical'[30].

**109**

**A lock of Arthur Hallam's hair**

Lady Elton Collection

Cat. 115

# 6. The Pyrenees

Tennyson's trip with Arthur Hallam to the Pyrenees in the summer of 1830 was the most important journey of his life. The expressed reason for going was to aid the Spanish exiles in their liberal cause with gifts of money, but, quickly disillusioned by the violent and anticlerical intentions of the revolutionaries, Tennyson turned to the landscape. Its austere, mountainous beauty provided the external images he needed to describe the interior landscape of his imagination. *The Lotos-Eaters* and *Mariana in the South* are two instances. Even the marvellous mountain landscape in 'Come down O maid from yonder mountain height', mingles memories of the Pyrenees with more immediate 1846 impressions of the Alps.

Tennyson twice returned to the Pyrenees, once in 1861, close to the period when John Stewart took his wonderful early photographs, and again in 1874. He found the place haunted with the presence of the past, as though Hallam's voice spoke with the noise of waters. In this late, and favourite lyric, he evokes, as so often, the power of the dead voice.

### In the Valley of Cauteretz

All along the valley, stream that flashest white,
Deepening thy voice with the deepening of the night,
All along the valley, where thy waters flow,
I walked with one I loved two and thirty years ago.
All along the valley, while I walked today,
The two and thirty years were a mist that rolls away;
For all along the valley, down thy rocky bed,
Thy living voice to me was as the voice of the dead,
And all along the valley, by rock and cave and tree,
O The voice of the dead was a living voice to me.

110
**John Stewart (d.1887)**
*Spanish Muleteers - at the Fair of Pau*
November 1853
Calotype [paper negative to paper positive], hand coloured
15.2 x 11 cms
National Museum of Photography, Film & Television (By courtesy of the Board of Trustees of the Science Museum)

111
**John Stewart**
*Le Pic du Midi de Bigorre*
No date
Albumen print 22.8 x 26.7 cms
National Museum of Photography, Film & Television (By courtesy of the Board of Trustees of the Science Museum)

112
**John Stewart**
*Eaux Chaudes. Pyrenees*
2 August 1852
Salted paper print 22.6 x 29 cms
National Museum of Photography, Film & Television (By courtesy of the Board of Trustees of the Science Museum)

112a
**John Stewart**
*Eaux Bonnes*
No date
Salted paper print 27.8 x 21.8
National Museum of Photography, Film & Television (By courtesy of the Board of Trustees of the Science Museum)

113
**John Stewart**
*Col d'Arrun, Pyrenees - et du pic du pont de Soubi*
No date
Salted paper print 23 x 29.5 cms
National Museum of Photography, Film & Television (By courtesy of the Board of Trustees of the Science Museum)

114
**John Stewart**
*Pic du Midi d'Ossau. Pyrenees. pris de la cabane du Col de Pombi*
2 September 1852
Salted paper print 22.6 x 27.5 cms
National Museum of Photography, Film & Television (By courtesy of the Board of Trustees of the Science Museum)

115
**John Stewart**
*Cirque de Gavarni, Pyrennes*
[1860s]
Albumen print 40.5 x 32 cms
National Museum of Photography, Film & Television (By courtesy of the Board of Trustees of the Science Museum)

Tennyson's sense of the place, as caught in *The Lotos Eaters*, is evoked in this photograph.

'Courage!' he said, and pointed toward the land,
'This mounting wave will roll us shoreward soon.'
In the afternoon they came unto a land
In which it seemed always afternoon.
All round the coast the languid air did swoon,
Breathing like one that hath a weary dream.
Full-faced above the valley stood the moon;

And like a downward smoke, the slender stream
Along the cliff to fall and pause and fall did seem.

A land of streams! some, like a downward smoke,
Slow-dropping veils of thinnest lawn, did go;
And some through wavering lights and shadows broke,
Rolling a slumbrous sheet of foam below.
They saw the gleaming river seaward flow
From the inner land: far off, three mountain-tops,
Three silent pinnacles of aged snow,
Stood sunset-flushed: and, dewed with showery drops,
Up-clomb the shadowy pine above the woven copse.

(*The Lotos Eaters*, 1-18)

## 116

### John Stewart

*The Corner of the [Blape Plante] at Pau with our House in the Centre*

No date

Salted paper print 17 x 20.2 cms

National Museum of Photography, Film & Television (By courtesy of the Board of Trustees of the Science Museum)

## 117

### Clarkson Stanfield (1793-1867)

Pic du Midi d'Ossau

1851

Watercolour and bodycolour over black chalk

47.5 x 34 cms

Trustees of the British Museum

Inscribed: 'Pic du Midi d'Ossau Saturday Nov' 9th 1851 Basses Pyrenees'

## 118

### John Harden (1772-1847)

*Travelling Companions*

Dated 10 September 1830

Sepia wash 13.2 x 20.8 cms

Trinity College, Cambridge

In September 1830, John Harden of Brathay Hall, Ambleside, and his family were on board the steamer from Bordeaux to Dublin, and, by chance, had as their companions Tennyson and Arthur Hallam. Harden made two sketches to record the occasion. This sketch shows, from left to right, Mr Robertson, the Misses Harden, Tennyson (in cape and hat) and Mr Glasgow. The second shows Mrs Ranken, the Misses Harden, Mr Glasgow, Mr Robertson, Arthur Hallam (reading a new 'Waverley' novel) and Tennyson, and is inscribed: 'Sketch taken on board the steamer, *Leeds* coming from Bordeaux to Dublin, 10 Sept. 1830, J.H.'. It is the only known picture showing Tennyson and Hallam together. Jessie Harden later recounted the meeting to Canon H.D. Rawnsley:

In the summer of 1830 my father, mother and sister, with myself spent the summer in the Pyrenees, and started from Bordeaux on 8th September in the steamer *Leeds* for Dublin. Our fellow passengers were four gentlemen - two of them Mr. Robertson, of Glasgow, and his cousin, of whom we know something through my mother's relatives, and two others who were none other than Mr. Tennyson and his friend Mr. Hallam. The weather was fine and we were sitting on deck. Mr. Hallam was a very interesting, delicate looking young man, and we saw nothing of him the first day; he was in the saloon. The second day was warm, and he came on deck, and kindly read to us some of Scott's novels, which had recently been published in one volume. We were all much charmed with our group of fellow-passengers. In my father's original pencil sketch Mr. Tennyson had a large cape, a tall hat, and a very decided nose[31].

# 7. The Lake District

## Mirehouse

In 1835 Tennyson sold the gold medal he won at Trinity College for £15, and on the proceeds paid his first visit to the Lake District, as the guest of his college friend James Spedding, whose family lived at Mirehouse on the shores of Bassenthwaite in the Lake District.

Cat. 121

**119**
**The Ven. Archdeacon R.H. Froude (1770-1859)**
*Mirehouse and Bassenthwaite Lake*
1802
Pencil and watercolour 37 x 22.5 cms
Spedding Collection

**120**
**The Ven. Archdeacon R.H. Froude**
*Mirehouse*
1802
Pencil and watercolour 36.5 x 22.9 cms
Spedding Collection

Robert Hurrell married Margaret Spedding, James's aunt. Their children included the historian James Anthony Froude. Mirehouse was built as a hunting lodge for the Earl of Derby in the early 18th century and had been left to John Spedding, James's father, by Thomas Storey in 1802.

**120a**
**Rev. Joseph Wilkinson (1764-1831)**
Mirehouse

1795
Watercolour 24.9 x 34.2 cms
The Wordsworth Trust

**121**
**Alfred Lord Tennyson**
Portrait by James Spedding
1835
Pencil and pastel 24.9 x 19 cms
Spedding Collection

Perhaps the nearest to the portrait by Samuel Laurence, showing the remarkable good looks of the young Tennyson. Spedding usually gives his drawings an intimate charm; here he includes the long pipe which was to be a pleasure to Tennyson throughout his life.

**122**
**Alfred Lord Tennyson**
Portrait by James Spedding
1835
Photograph after drawing 11 x 19 cms
Spedding Collection

James shows Tennyson in his cloak beside the fireside at Mirehouse (the actual chair in which he sits is exhibited below). Tennyson's short-sightedness is emphasised by the way in which he holds the book close to his face.

**123**
**Chair**
110 x 63.5 cms
Spedding Collection
The chair shown in the above portrait.

**124**
**Alfred Lord Tennyson**
Portrait by Edward Fitzgerald
1835
Pencil 18 x 11 cms
Spedding Collection

A backward view of the poet showing his head bent forward and his tousled hair. Doubtless he is once more reading a book. This table is still at Mirehouse.

**125**
**Chair**
c. 1800
Cane 81 cms x 55 cms
Spedding Collection
The chair shown in the above portrait.

126
**Edward Fitzgerald (1809-1883)**
Portrait by James Spedding
*c.* 1831
Pencil 33 x 24.5 cms
Spedding Collection

Cat. 127

127
**Edward Fitzgerald**
Portrait by James Spedding
1835
Pen and grey wash with pink crayon
27.9 x 18.7 cms
Spedding Collection

The table at which Fitzgerald sits is still to be seen at Mirehouse.

128
**Edward Fitzgerald**
Portrait by James Spedding
1835
Pencil 15.3 x 11.5 cms
Spedding Collection

Although he was a contemporary of his at Cambridge, Tennyson only became a friend of Edward Fitzgerald on his visit to Mirehouse. Fitzgerald, a school fellow of Spedding's at Bury St Edmunds and later famous for his translation of the *Rubaiyat of Omar Khayyam* 1859, was immediately struck by Tennyson's talent; on 23 May he wrote to John Allen:

I will say no more of Tennyson than that the more I see of him, the more cause I have to think him great . . . I must however say, further, that I felt what Charles Lamb describes, a sense of depression at times from the overshadowing of a so much more lofty intellect than my own.

In Tennyson's itinerant days before his marriage, Fitzgerald often shared his London lodgings with Tennyson, and as the poem below shows, encouraged him with his praise. In later years Fitzgerald was hurt by what he took to be Tennyson's neglect of their friendship, but in 1883 Tennyson wrote Fitzgerald the affectionate poem, *To E. Fitzgerald*. Unfortunately, to Tennyson's regret, Fitzgerald died before receiving the verses.

Old Fitz, who from your suburb grange,
Where once I tarried for a while,
Glance at the wheeling Orb of change,
And greet it with a kindly smile;
Whom yet I see as there you sit
Beneath your sheltering garden-tree,
And while your doves about you flit,
And plant on shoulder, hand and knee,
Or on your head their rosy feet,
As if they knew your diet spares
Whatever moved in that full sheet
Let down to Peter at his prayers;
Who live on milk and meal and grass;
And once for ten long weeks I tried
Your table of Pythagoras,
And seemed at first 'a thing enskied'
(As Shakespeare has it) airy-light
To float above the ways of men,
Then fell from that half-spiritual height
Chilled, till I tasted flesh again
One night when earth was winter-black,
And all the heavens flashed in frost;
And on me, half-asleep, came back
That wholesome heat the blood had lost,
And set me climbing icy capes
And glaciers, over which there rolled
To meet me long-armed vines with grapes
Of Eshcol hugeness; for the cold
Without, and warmth within me, wrought
To mould the dream; but none can say
That Lenten fare makes Lenten thought,
Who reads your golden Eastern lay,
Than which I know no version done
In English more divinely well;
A planet equal to the sun
Which cast it, that large infidel
Your Omar; and your Omar drew
Full-handed plaudits from our best
In modern letters, and from two,
Old friends outvaluing all the rest,
Two voices heard on earth no more;
But we old friends are still alive,
And I am nearing seventy-four,
While you have touched at seventy-five
And so I send a birthday line

Of greeting; and my son, who dipt
In some forgotten book of mine
With sallow scraps of manuscript,
And dating many a year ago,
Has hit on this, which you will take
My Fitz, and welcome, as I know
Less for its own than for the sake
Of one recalling gracious times,
When, in our younger London days,
You found some merit in my rhymes,
And I more pleasure in your praise.

**129**
**Emily Lady Tennyson (1813-96)**
Journal
Holograph manuscript
Lincolnshire County Council:
Tennyson Research Centre, Lincoln

Emily Tennyson's journal was written after
Tennyson's death to aid Hallam Tennyson in his
writing of the *Memoir*. In this extract, Emily,
rather oddly writing in the third person, describes
her first meeting with Tennyson's old friend at
Mirehouse.

'Myer House
    James Spedding discovered that they were at an Hotel
in Keswick called on them and pressed them to go to
Myer House. Her first acquaintance with this good &
wise & delightful friend
    Most kind was their reception and their visit very
pleasant; Excursions on lake and mountain which they
enjoyed and the family circle which could not fail to be
interesting. The father a 'fine old English Gentleman'
and the brother Tom looking as if he had walked down
from some stately picture of Velasquez'.

## Tennyson and William Wordsworth

The Speddings had long been acquainted with the
Wordsworth family. John Spedding, James's father,
had sat with the poet on the same school bench at
Hawkshead Grammar School, the two being exact
contemporaries. James had met Wordsworth on the
occasion of giving his prize oration in Trinity
College Chapel. No wonder then, that Spedding
should take Tennyson to meet the poet that they
both admired at his home at Rydal Mount.
Wordsworth's visitors' book records the meeting,
and allows one to correct an impression left by
Fitzgerald's letters that they decided not to call.

    Tennyson was profoundly influenced by his
great predecessor, and, after a short period of
doubt, his admiration was reciprocated. When
Tennyson met Wordsworth in 1842 in London, he
found it difficult to talk, but finally Rogers
arranged in 1845 that they be at dinner together and

tactfully arranged for Wordsworth to come back
into the room to have a private word with
Tennyson and to allow the younger man to express
his gratitude for Wordsworth's work. Wordsworth
expressed his pleasure to his American friend
Henry Reed:

I saw Tennyson when I was in London several times. He
is decidedly the first of our living Poets, and I hope will
live to give the world still better things. You will be
pleased to hear that he expressed in the strongest terms
his gratitude to my writings. To this I was far from
indifferent, though persuaded that he is not much in
sympathy with what I should myself most value in my
attempts, viz. the spirituality with which I have
endeavoured to invest the material Universe and the
moral relation under which I have wished to exhibit its
most ordinary appearances.

At about the same time Wordsworth told another
visitor to Rydal Mount, Thomas Cooper, the
Chartist, that he considered Tennyson had as fine
a sense of music in syllables 'as Keats and Milton'.
Further evidence of Tennyson's admiration comes
from the Reverend H. Montague Butler, Master of
Trinity College. He noted that Tennyson never
spoke of Wordsworth without 'marked reverence',
while he would 'qualify his admiration for Robert
Browning's genius', and although he did have some
surprising judgments of Wordsworth's poetry (he
thought, for instance, that *Tintern Abbey* could be
shorter), his admiration was indeed fixed, and is
symbolised by his including Wordsworth as one of
the carved heads on his fireplace at Aldworth, the
other figures being Homer, Dante, Chaucer,
Spenser and Milton. Wordsworth is the only
contemporary to be included.

**130**
**William Wordsworth (1770-1850)**
Portrait by James Spedding
*c.*1836
Pencil 12.7 x 10.2 cms
The Wordsworth Trust

The portrait bears the caption 'Wordsworth -
Sketched by Mr Spedding at the Colonial Office
G.B.'

**131**
**Francis Turner Palgrave (1824-97)**
Letter to Christopher Wordsworth
20 July 1851
The Wordsworth Trust

Perhaps the least known tribute that Tennyson
made to Wordsworth was his overseeing Palgrave's
selection of the Wordsworth poems in his *Golden
Treasury*. In a letter to Christopher Wordsworth,

the poet's nephew and biographer, Palgrave wrote:

Dear Sir

I find from the Publisher that a copy of a little Anthology I have made with A Tennyson's help (the Golden Treasury) has been sent to you. This was owing to a general direction of mine that the book schd. go to the Copywright proprietors who had allowed me to collect from their stores: but as the permission in case of your illustrious uncle was obtained by one of Moxon's partners I am not sure whether it is to you that I am indebted.

I therefore send this note in explanation.

You will see that WW. has given us more numerically & quantitively than any other poet. That our selection from him was not twice as long as it is, was due partly to the fact that several magnificent things like Hartleap Well & Laodamia appeared more properly *narrative* than *lyrical*: partly to Tennyson's own strong feeling that we shd. admit nothing which did not exhibit his honoured predecessor in his fullest strength & glory.

Cat. 124

132
**Rydal Mount Visitors Book**
1830-1847
The Wordsworth Trust

Under the month of May the two names are entered:

Mr. J. Spedding     Mirehouse
Mr. A. Tennyson  London

133
**William Westall (1781-1850)**
Rydal Mount
1831
Watercolour
The Wordsworth Trust

Tennyson later told his son of how he climbed Loughrigg and, looking down at Rydal, thought to himself, 'never was a poet more comfortably housed'[32].

Tennyson was always very upset by hostile reviews, and hated publishing his works. Before 1850, when, as Poet Laureate, he began to develop a public voice, poetry was still an essentially private matter. In 1838, Milnes wrote: 'Tennyson composes every day, but nothing will persuade him to print, or even write it down'.

Nevertheless, his standing as the finest poet of his generation was established by three publications. *Poems, Chiefly Lyrical* (1830) included 'Mariana' and 'The Kraken'; *Poems* (1833) contained 'The Lady of Shalott', 'Oenone' and 'The Lotos-Eaters'. *Poems* (1842) was to become the best-loved collection of his poems, and secured his reputation. It included 'Ulysses', 'Morte d'Arthur', 'St Simeon Stylites' and 'Break, break, break'.

**134**

**Alfred Lord Tennyson**
*Poems*
First edition
London: Edward Moxon, 1833
Lincolnshire County Council:
Tennyson Research Centre, Lincoln

**135**

**Alfred Lord Tennyson**
*Poems in Two Volumes*
London: Edward Moxon, 1842
Lincolnshire County Council:
Tennyson Research Centre, Lincoln

'Ulysses', contained in this volume, was composed within a month of Tennyson's hearing of Hallam's death. It was, said Tennyson, 'about the need of going forward and braving the struggle of life perhaps more simply than anything in *In Memoriam*'. Another time he commented, 'There is more about myself in 'Ulysses', which was written under the sense of loss and that all had gone by, but that still life must be fought out to the end'. Certainly, for Ulysses, the first hero of Tennyson's great monologues based on subjects from ancient classical times, all had gone by. Ulysses is an old man, and weary with ordinary day-to-day life. It was in the past that life was exciting when he

drunk delight of battle with [his] peers,
Far on the ringing plains of windy Troy.

There is in Ulysses, as in Tennyson in his grief, a yearning for the past, and alongside this, a yearning for change, for the future, and a dislike of the present moment. The aged Ulysses, having after twenty years attained his desire and come

home, cannot rest there. He needs something more,
To sail beyond the sunset, and the baths
Of all the western stars, until I die.

Indeed, death may be (and will be) the cost of setting off again, taking on life as challenge. For Tennyson, to continue to write, to try to write well and to live up to the high poetic expectations that Hallam had had for him was also endeavour and struggle, life to be 'fought out to the end'. But through the long lines of high ambition in *Ulysses* we feel the sway of weariness. The intention 'not to yield' is undermined by the rhythms of defeat, and yet the very choice of Ulysses as hero announces Tennyson's strength and resolution to continue. Ulysses, after all, was a subject for Homer, for Dante, for Shakespeare, and - in another medium - for Tennyson's older contemporary J.M.W. Turner; but that Tennyson also chose him reveals his wish ultimately to, as it were, justify Hallam's high regard: to challenge, and to place himself amongst the highest poetic company.

**136**

**Alfred Lord Tennyson**
*Locksley Hall*
*c.*1837-8
Holograph manuscript
Trinity College, Cambridge

Tennyson noted: 'The whole poem represents young life, its good side, its deficiencies, and its yearnings.'

Tennyson had been told by Henry Hallam that 'the English people liked verse in trochaics' and that helped persuade Tennyson to use the metre. Again, Tennyson's apostle friend, R.C. Trench used the metre in the poem *Sabbation* (1838).

Though the poem is another example of Tennyson's providing a dramatic form to express an adolescent anxiety over being rejected in love, the poem has a grandeur in its petulance linked with ideals of internationalism - 'the parliament of man'. With the racism of the time he speaks of the Africans with their 'narrow foreheads'. Jowett once noted that the poem, though distanced from Tennyson himself by the narrative device of a speaker, seemed to portray many of Tennyson's own opinions.

Jowett said of the poem:

"Locksley Hall,", although spoken in the character of a disappointed lover, contains the sum of his politics when he was a young man, and though he wrote an epilogue to the poem sixty years later, the point of view from which he regarded the world in this poem was never really altered, but only underwent the natural change of old age. The daily and weekly movements of politics, which, like the weather, are always changing, made little or no impression on him; the weight of the unknown seemed to fall upon him more heavily.[33]

**137**
**Alfred Lord Tennyson**
*Oenone*
*c.*1830-2
Holograph manuscript
Trinity College, Cambridge

First published in 1832. The word coinages of that early version, its "cedarshadowy valleys", its "loud glenriver" and "snowycolumned range", give way to the less elaborate vocabulary of the poem we know in its revised version of 1842.

The famous story of love and destruction, the awarding by Paris of the prize, the beautiful fruit of 'gleaming rind', not to Hera, Queen of Heaven, who could offer power; not to Pallas, Goddess of Wisdom, who could offer self-conquest; but to Aphrodite, Goddess of Love, who could offer 'the fairest and most loving wife in Greece'. That wife was Helen, and the choice led to the Trojan War. Tennyson tells the classic story obliquely, from the point of view of forgotten Oenone, the river nymph, Paris' former love. She must tell her story 'ere I die', but though she obsessively tells it, and is another abandoned maid, she is not Mariana; Tennyson allows her the energy of vengeful thoughts. She wants to meet 'The Abominable' who set Paris up as Judge:

> that I might speak my mind,
> And tell her to her face how much I hate
> Her presence.

"I will not die alone", she threatens:

> I will rise and go
> Down into Troy, and ere the stars come forth
> Talk with the wild Cassandra, for she says
> A fire dances before her, and a sound
> Rings ever in her ears of armed men.

Earlier, when the three great Goddesses had come down for judgement

> At their feet the crocus brake like fire.

It is part of Tennyson's pattern that this fire of spring and growth should turn into its catastrophic opposite, the fire that burnt Troy. The shadow had been there all the time, even as Oenone remembered the former "fruitful kisses" of Paris, that had come like "quick-falling dew",

> thick as Autumn rains
> Flash in the pools of whirling Simois.

The mention of the Simois in this happy context is a dark omen, for the Simois was the river of Troy.

It is all there: the love that is doomed, irrecoverable and painfully fresh in the memory. Tennyson was to express this sense of 'Death in Life' again and again.

**138**
**Alfred Lord Tennyson**
*The Gardener's Daughter*
*c.*1833-4
Holograph manuscript
Trinity College, Cambridge

Tennyson declared:

The centre of the poem, that passage describing the girl (lines 124-40), must be full and rich. The poem is so, to a fault, especially the descriptions of nature, for the lover is an artist, but, this being so, the central picture must hold its place.

Even so, Tennyson admired his own 'descriptions of nature'. He told C.V. Stanford, the composer, that 'he considered the best line he ever wrote to be "The mellow ouzel fluted in the elm' (line 93).

Aubrey de Vere records finding Tennyson with the manuscript of the poem:

The poet had corrected it as carefully as he had originally composed it in his head, where he was in the habit of keeping more than one poem at a time before he wrote down any of them.

Interestingly, though Tennyson was reluctant to publish (the poem was written nine years before it appeared in 1842), he shared his writing process with his friends. He explained to Aubrey De Vere that he was going to delete forty lines:

The corrections jostled each other, and the poem seemed out of gear. Spedding has just now remarked that it wants nothing but that this passage, forty lines, should be omitted. He is right.

**139**
**Alfred Lord Tennyson**
*The Two Voices*
*c.*1833-4
Holograph manuscript
Trinity College, Cambridge

**140**
**Alfred Lord Tennyson**
'Oh! that 'twere possible'
*c.*1833-4
Holograph manuscript
Trinity College, Cambridge

Benjamin Jowett, Master of Balliol College, Oxford, wrote to Hallam Tennyson after the death of his father:

He once asked which I thought the most touching lines in any of his works. I venture to reply the lines in

"Maud", beginning:
O that 'twere possible,
After long grief and pain
To find the arms of my true love
Round me once again!

He gave some sign of assent to the answer, adding, by the way, that they were not originally meant for that place.[34]

The earliest manuscript was written soon after Hallam's death. The direct expression of longing, the exclamatory style, the calling up of the past in simple words and true rhymes, all make this poem one of the most immediate of Tennyson's accounts of loss. It is the first poem after Hallam's death that evokes the sense that Tennyson was to have for so many years - of being haunted:

A shadow flits before me,
Not thou, but like to thee

. . . .

It leads me forth at evening,
It lightly winds and steals. . .

141
**Alfred Lord Tennyson**
*Edwin Morris*
1839
Holograph Manuscript
Trinity College, Cambridge

Edwin Morris, written 1839 and published 1851, draws on some of the overflow lines from *The Gardener's Daughter*. It is a poem which seems to reflect Tennyson's unhappy falling in love with Rosa Baring; it is on the theme of lovers separated by relatives. As in 'Locksley Hall' the hero is betrayed by mercenary brothers and cousins. Against this world of high passion touched with melodrama, Tennyson places the clerk, Edward Bull, who obstinately believes in woman's functional and subsidiary role:

I say, God made the woman for the man,
And for the good and increase of the world.

142
**Alfred Lord Tennyson**
*The Princess*
London: Moxon 1847
Lincolnshire County Council:
Tennyson Research Centre, Lincoln

Here is a medley, as Tennyson called this extraordinary mixture of tale, teaching and song, whose heroine is poles away from the ladies who had featured in Tennyson's earlier verse. Here is no depressed Mariana stuck in deathly desire, no abandoned Oenone telling her story ''ere I die'. The lady of *The Princess* does not absorb any of the 'feminine' passive feelings of her creator; she

is energetic, ambitious for learning, sees that women must exercise their talents in separation before entering in equality the world of men. Rather comically, and on something like the pattern of the young men in Shakespeare's *Love's Labour's Lost*, she sets about an exclusively feminine academy of learning, with lectures on history, science, literature from 'thundrous Epic' to

Jewels five-words-long
That on the stretched forefinger of all Time
Sparkle forever
(II, 355-7)

From debates 'mixt with inmost terms / Of art and science' (II, 423-4) students move to practical geology,

Hammering and clinking, chattering stony names
Of shale and hornblende, rag and trap and tuff,
Amygdaloid and trachyte, till the Sun
Grew broader toward his death and fell, and all
The rosy heights came out above the lawns
(III, 343-7)

The other sex, as in Shakespeare's comedy, inevitably penetrates this calm world where reason and learning reign. The masculine desire for love is bolstered by the songs sung and read by some of the ladies in their moments of leisure. These are lyrics of feeling, ranging from the sadness, even anguish of 'Tears, idle tears', to the seductive invitation of 'Now sleeps the crimson petal, now the white', and its companion in persuasion 'Come down, O maid, from yonder mountain height'. Of course, the Princess yields, though not without a bloody, near mortal struggle, and Reason and Feeling unite in marriage. This is not capitulation, but wholeness. The Prince appreciates the exchange, and sees the richness it promises:

Breathe upon my brows;
In that fine air I tremble, all the past
Melts mist-like into this bright hour, and this
Is morn to more, and all the rich to-come
Reels, as the golden Autumn woodland reels
Athwart the smoke of burning weeds.
(VII, 332-7)

The whole strange tale is set within the framework of a Victorian house party, surely an invitation to readers to apply the story to their own times. A young Queen was the foremost person in this country and monarch of a large Empire. It was time to do something about the education of women and Tennyson was among the first men to realise this.

143
**Alfred Lord Tennyson**
Letter to James Spedding
Early October 1834
Lincolnshire County Council:
Tennyson Research Centre, Lincoln

My dear James

It may be you have waited some time for a reply - but you lie - you haven't waited so say no more. I have been out, or you should have heard from me before this. So, I pray you, make not any little lapse of time that may possibly have slided away into the unrecoverable between the writing of your letter and the receipt of mine, precendent for further delay in answering this. For your letters do my moral and intellectual man much good. I am going to town with Emily to-morrow and I expect a token from you on my return. You ask me what I have been doing - I have written several things I saw you . . . but you can scarcely expect me to write them out for you: for I can scarcely bring myself to write them out for myself and do you think I love you better than myself? I had thought your Paley had taught you better. By a quaint coincidence I received your letter directed (I suppose) by Philip van Artevelde with Philip himself (not the man but the book) and I wish to tell you that I think him a noble fellow. I close in him in most that he says of modern poetry though it may be that he does not take sufficiently into consideration the *peculiar* strength evolved by such writers as Byron and Shelley which however mistaken they may be did yet give the world another heart and new pulses - and so are we kept going. Blessed be those that grease the wheels of the old world, insomuch as to move on is better than to stand still. But 'Philip is a famous man' and makes me shamed of my own faults. Apropos of faults I have corrected much of my last volume and if you would send me your copy I would insert my corrections. Heaven knows what Douglas brought you: as for some stanzas about a corridor I know not whether there be such a poem: if there be it is very evident you have it not rightly.

I think on second thoughts though much against my will I will write thee out a poem partly because Charles likes it, partly to give a local habitation on this paper and in your brainpeace to what lese flies loosely through the wind of my own memory like a Sibyl's leaf. Voilà! be merciful.

'I have written several things . . . but you can scarcely expect me to write them out for you: for I can scarcely bring myself to write them out for myself and do you think I love you better than myself?' The letter is an indication of how Tennyson saw poetry less as possible material for publication than as an essentially private pursuit shared between friends. Earlier at Mirehouse Spedding's father had remarked, 'Well, Mr F[itzgerald], and what is it? Mr Tennyson reads, and Jem criticises; - is that it?'[35]

Cat. 13   "The Poet Laureate" by 'Ape'

Cat. 12   *Mr Tennyson reading 'In Memoriam' to his Sovereign*

Cat. 32  Tennyson by Frederick Sandys

Cat. 41   George Tennyson by Lawrence

Cat. 42   Mary Tennyson by John Russell

Cat. 43   Elizabeth Russell by John Russell

Cat. 45   Elizabeth Tennyson by unknown artist

Cat. 44   George Clayton Tennyson by unknown artist

Cat. 88   Arthur Henry Hallam by Sir Arthur Martin Shee

Pic du Midi d'Ossau.
Saturday Nov 3rd 1851.
Bases Pyrenees.

Cat. 117  Pic du Midi d'Ossau by Clarkson Stanfield

Cat. 120a  Mirehouse by Rev. Joseph Wilkinson

Cat. 155  Coniston Water with Tent Lodge by J.M.W. Turner

Cat. 156  Emily Tennyson by G.F. Watts

Tennyson by Samuel Laurence

Cat. 172  Queen Victoria by F. Winterhalter        Cat. 171  Prince Albert by F. Winterhalter

Cat. 205  Elaine by E.H. Corbould

William Wordsworth by Benjamin Robert Haydon (1842)

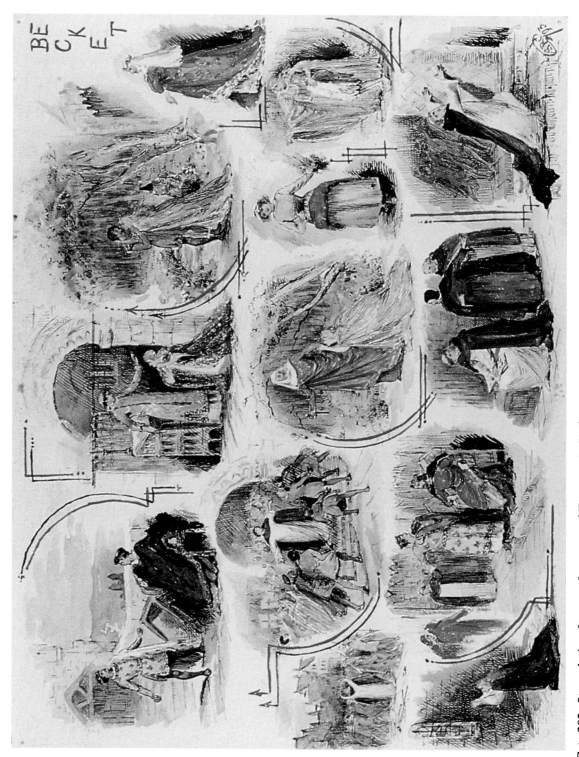

Cat. 282  Stage design for a performance of Tennyson's *Becket*

Cat. 293 Mariana by Dante Gabriel Rossetti

Cat. 322  Lancelot at the Chapel of the Holy Grail by Edward Burne-Jones

Cat. 320  The Rift in the Lute by Arthur Hughes

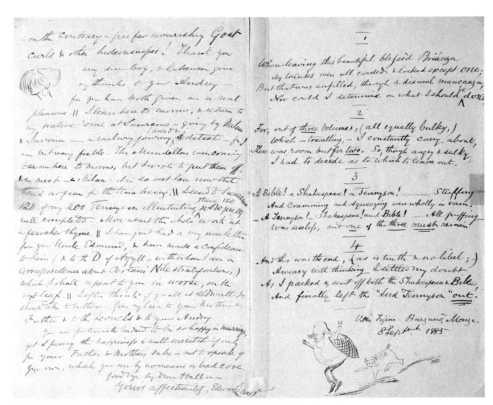

Cat. 334 Letter from Edward Lear to Emily Tennyson

Cat. 331 'Faringford' by Edward Lear

Cat. 336  Untitled landscape by Edward Lear

Cat. 335  Enoch Arden's Island by Edward Lear

Cat. 227  The Valley of the Shadow of Death by Roger Fenton

Cat. 228  Lord Raglan by Roger Fenton

Cat. 230 Officers of the Fourth Light Dragoons by Roger Fenton

Cat. 231  Photographic Van by Roger Fenton

Cat. 356  Thomas Carlyle by Julia Margaret Cameron

Cat. 365  Sir Henry Taylor by Julia Margaret Cameron

Cat. 360  Robert Browning by Julia Margaret Cameron

Cat. 358  George Frederic Watts by Julia Margaret Cameron

In 1850 Tennyson married, published *In Memoriam*, and succeeded Wordsworth as Poet Laureate to Queen Victoria.

These three events were very closely connected. The decision to publish the elegies of *In Memoriam*, and to preface them with that late poem (1848) asserting a firm faith, 'Strong Son of God, immortal Love', must have cleared the way finally for marriage. In publishing, Tennyson in some part let go of the past, and by an assertion of faith preceding the doubts and darknesses of the poem, he made public a firmness in his religious position. Emily, who had loved Tennyson constantly for fourteen years, must have felt encouraged. A future was possible (as indeed it is at the end of *In Memoriam* itself, with its finale of marriage). Tennyson and Emily married and the Laureateship quickly followed, for the poem was an unprecedented success and caught the national imagination in a way that no poetry had done since Byron.

## In Memoriam

144
**Alfred Lord Tennyson**
*In Memoriam*
1842
Holograph manuscript
Lincolnshire County Council:
Tennyson Research Centre, Lincoln

From 1833 to 1850, a period of continual solitude and great personal hardship Tennyson's secret pre-occupations were the accumulating elegiac lyrics, 133 in number, which make up *In Memoriam*. The poem is obsessional, haunting, both bitter and pious. It is the more faithful because of its own doubts, the more popular because its learning was of a public and easy kind. No poet had ever sifted the language for so sustained a melancholy timbre. Tennyson confronts the sense of loss, not so that he can show pain, but so that he might make a music that is best decoded as a kind of celebration.

145
**Coventry Patmore (1823-96)**
Letter to Alfred Lord Tennyson
9 May 1893
Lincolnshire County Council:
Tennyson Research Centre, Lincoln

Tennyson often mislaid his manuscripts, and in 1848 left the 'butcher's account book' manuscript of *In Memoriam* in a cupboard in his temporary lodgings in London. He asked Coventry Patmore, a young friend and disciple, to recover it.

Dear Lord Tennyson,

I fear that I have no letters from your Father, having given them away, at various times to friends who wanted autographs. The letter concerning the MS. of "In Memoriam", I gave to the late Sir John Simeon, thinking that he ought to have it, as he had the manuscript itself. This letter asked me to visit the lodging in Mornington Place, Hampstead Road, which he had occupied two or three weeks before, and to try to recover the MS. which he had left behind in a closet where he was used to keep some of his provisions. The landlady said that no such book had been left, but I insisted in looking for it myself, and found it where your father said it was.

With my best respects to your mother
Yours faithfully
Coventry Patmore

Cat. 144

146
**Alfred Lord Tennyson**
*In Memoriam*
London: Edward Moxon, 1850 (proof copy)
Lincolnshire County Council:
Tennyson Research Centre, Lincoln

In March 1850, Moxon issued a number of proof copies of *In Memoriam* which Tennyson sent to several of his friends for their comments. He was adamant that, once read, these trial copies should be destroyed. In the copy he gave to Edmund Lushington he wrote: 'Essentially & inconceivably private till its later tho longer brother appear then to die the death by Fire! Mind! A.T.'[36]

This is one of only three surviving copies. The title page is almost identical with the first edition, except that the typeface of the title is smaller and the printer's name is placed in the middle of the page. Further, the dedication before page one reads *In Memoriam A.H.H. Obiit Sept MDCCCXXXIII*. The pencil note at the front of the volume declares that the title page is 'inserted & is from the first published edition'. The volume is a gift to Tennyson from G L Craik on behalf of Macmillans, to whom Tennyson wrote:

I thank you and the Macmillans for your chivalrous gift [the proof sheets of *In Memoriam* and *Maud*]. I value this more especially as showing your abhorrence for the sale of proof sheets. Yours gratefully Tennyson March - 1891.

Besides Lushington, whose marriage to his sister Cecilia in October 1842 was the inspiration behind the concluding poem, Tennyson gave proof copies to G.S. Venables, Aubrey De Vere, James Spedding and Drummond Rawnsley.

The text is open at poem VII:

Fair ship that from the Italian shore
 Sailest the placid ocean-plains
 With my lost Arthur's loved remains,
Spread thy full wings, and waft him o'er.

So draw him home to those that mourn
 In vain; a favourable speed
 Ruffle thy mirrored mast, and lead
Through prosperous floods his holy urn.

All night no ruder air perplex
 Thy sliding keel, till Phosphor, bright
 As our pure love, through early light
Shall glimmer on the dewy decks.

Sphere all your lights around, above;
 Sleep, gentle heavens, before the prow;
 Sleep, gentle winds, as he sleeps now,
My friend, the brother of my love;

My Arthur, whom I shall not see
 Till all my widowed race be run;
 Dear as the mother to the son,
More than my brothers are to me.

The poem is an address to an inanimate object, and it is part of the ritual of mourning to want, in imagination if not in fact, to be involved with the detail of funeral. This is a prayer for a calm passage home: the ship carrying the body becomes a protective bird and the harmony of the entire universe is invoked. Night, dawn, the star of morning, all the stars, the winds, the sky, the sea, all will collaborate; even the decks of the ship will have the freshness of dew upon them. The love of the universe expresses the love of the poet, and the intensity of this love becomes clear in the last verse.

## 147
## Alfred Lord Tennyson
*In Memoriam*
London: Edward Moxon, 1850
Lincolnshire County Council:
Tennyson Research Centre, Lincoln

This is the first edition, and the seventh poem is now 'Dark House', a late addition to the sequence:

Dark house, by which once more I stand
 Here in the long unlovely street,
 Doors, where my heart was used to beat
So quickly, waiting for a hand,

A hand that can be clasped no more -
 Behold me, for I cannot sleep,
 And like a guilty thing I creep
At earliest morning to the door.

He is not here; but far away
 The noise of life begins again,
 And ghastly through the drizzling rain
On the bald street breaks the blank day.

Life is mere noise, day breaks to blankness and meaninglessness in rain, and the house is dark. There is no comment on the grief, no analysis, just the presentation of the facts. 'He is not here': the sentence, cruelly brief, insists upon absence, while the living man, haunting his hope and his past, has become himself a ghost creeping to the door like 'a guilty thing' (the phrase used of the ghost in *Hamlet*). Tennyson's poem takes its place in the classical tradition of addresses to the houses, and the doors of houses, of absent beloveds, most notably, in English, Chaucer's Troilus, who addresses the 'colde dores' of the 'paleys empty and disconsolat' after Criseyde has left for the Greek camp. But where Troilus almost sings in the rhetoric of grief, Tennyson's power is in his restraint; in the pattern of his words the remorseless monosyllables thud out the message of absence and meaninglessness.

At the foot of the page, in the handwriting of Francis Palgrave (the one-time owner) the accolade 'perfect' is written. Palgrave has not hesitated to criticise his friend's verse on the opposite page, where he writes, 'I think there is a little feebleness in the sound of 'and unto me no second friend'.

148

**Alfred Lord Tennyson**

*In Memoriam*

London: Edward Moxon, 1850

Lincolnshire County Council:

Tennyson Research Centre, Lincoln

Open at poem II:

Old Yew, which graspest at the stones
 That name the under-lying dead,
 Thy fibres net the dreamless head,
Thy roots are wrapt about the bones.

The seasons bring the flower again,
 And bring the firstling to the flock;
 And in the dusk of thee, the clock
Beats out the little lives of men.

O not for thee the glow, the bloom,
 Who changest not in any gale,
 Nor branding summer Suns avail
To touch thy thousand years of gloom:

And gazing on thee, sullen tree,
 Sick for thy stubborn hardihood,
 I seem to fail from out my blood
And grow incorporate into thee.

The absorption with death takes on an almost physical intensity; the churchyard tree seems to be holding the dead in a loving and enviable embrace, yet it is uncaring about the time that beats out the measure of man's life, and, in a different sense, beats out his life. Variously in this short poem Tennyson suggests that there is no feeling that does not move in at least two directions: he can, for example, be at once sick for, yearning to have, such a stolid carelessness to feeling as the tree has, and at the same time sicken at such seemingly permanent indifference. To grow incorporate into the tree suggests the physical and the non-human. It would mean death, and yet there is a hovering suggestion, through the very word 'incorporate', of the incorporeal, even the spiritual.

149

**Alfred Lord Tennyson**

*In Memoriam*

London: Edward Moxon, 1850

Lincolnshire County Council:

Tennyson Research Centre, Lincoln

Open at poem XCV:

By night we lingered on the lawn
 For underfoot the herb was dry;
 And genial warmth; and o'er the sky
The silvery haze of summer drawn;

And calm that let the tapers burn
 Unwavering: not a cricket chirred:
 The brook alone far-off was heard,
And on the board the fluttering urn:

And bats went round in fragrant skies,
 And wheeled or lit the filmy shapes
 That haunt the dusk with ermine capes
And woolly breasts and beaded eyes;

While now we sang old songs that pealed
 From knoll to knoll, where, couched at ease,
 The white kine glimmered, and the trees
Laid their dark arms about the field.

But when those others, one by one,
 Withdrew themselves from me and night,
 And in the house light after light
Went out, and I was all alone,

A hunger seized my heart; I read
 Of that glad year which once had been,
 In those fallen leaves which kept their green,
The noble letters of the dead:

And strangely on the silence broke
 The silent-speaking words, and strange
 Was love's dumb cry defying change
To test his worth; and strangely spoke

The faith, the vigour, bold to dwell
 On doubts that drive the coward back,
 And keen through wordy snares to track
Suggestion to her inmost cell.

So word by word, and line by line,
 The dead man touched me from the past,
 And all at once it seemed at last
The living soul was flashed on mine,

And mine in this was wound, and whirled
 About empyreal heights of thought,
 And came on that which is, and caught
The deep pulsations of the world,

Aeonian music measuring out
 The steps of Time - the shocks of Chance -
 The blows of Death. At length my trance
Was cancelled, stricken through with doubt.

Vague words! but ah, how hard to frame
 In matter-moulded forms of speech,
 Or even for intellect to reach
Through memory that which I became:

Till now the doubtful dusk revealed
 The knolls once more where, couched at ease,
 The white kine glimmered, and the trees
Laid their dark arms about the field:

And sucked from out the distant gloom
 A breeze began to tremble o'er
 The large leaves of the sycamore,
And fluctuate all the still perfume,

And gathering freshlier overhead,
 Rocked the full-foliaged elms, and swung
 The heavy-folded rose, and flung
The lilies to and fro, and said

'The dawn, the dawn,' and died away
 And East and West, without a breath,
 Mixt their dim lights, like life and death
To broaden into boundless day.

An intimation of immortality; an answer, in a way to the quest of *In Memoriam*. And it came to Tennyson, as mystic experiences do, as a gift, a grace. Tennyson describes a calm summer night out of doors, with tea and talk and family songs. This is his home world: a lawn, and a group of known people who feel at ease in a loved and loving landscape:

> and the trees
> Laid their dark arms about the field.

This social group emphasises the subsequent solitude when the poet, alone and hungry for the past, has a deeper experience. The letters of the dead Hallam are leaves fallen yet green; in their 'silent-speaking' they evoke a similarly paradoxical yearning, a 'dumb cry', and somehow, at last, the hunger is fed. The physical man is dead but the soul that 'at once' flashed on Tennyson's is living, and in a kind of trance there is for the poet an apprehension of the certainty of absolute being:

> And came on that which is, and caught
> The deep pulsations of the world . . .

Morning comes and dispels a gloom, a doubt about that mystic certainty that had settled on the poet, and this time the message comes not from any 'living soul' but from the whole natural world itself. The green leaves that give fresh inspiration are not Hallam's actual letters now, but the large leaves of the sycamore moved by a breeze, a sign itself of inspiration. The breeze rocks trees and flowers to light and perfume, and dawn comes and offers a silent revelation, a message; it is made up of oppositions, but there is an assurance, a certainty about it:

> And East and West, without a breath,
> Mixt their dim lights, like life and death,
> To broaden into boundless day.

## 150
**Alfred Gatty D.D.**
*A Key to Tennyson's In Memoriam*
London: George Bell & Sons, 1882
Lincolnshire County Council:
Tennyson Research Centre, Lincoln

Gatty looks for the literary sources of the language and sentiments of *In Memoriam*, but Tennyson's irritable annotations deny most of his conclusions. Clearly he regarded such critical explorations as something of an impertinence.

# Marriage

## 151
**Alfred Lord Tennyson**
Letter to Catherine Rawnsley
25 December 1849
Lincolnshire County Council:
Tennyson Research Centre, Lincoln

The Rawnsleys were friends and neighbours of the Somersby Tennysons. Catherine was the cousin of Emily Sellwood, soon to be Emily Tennyson. She was the orphaned niece of Emily's uncle, Sir John Franklin, the Arctic explorer. Tennyson and she met at the marriage of Tennyson's favourite brother Charles to Emily's sister Louisa in 1836, and were, perhaps for a moment, attracted to each other, but it was Emily who became the centre of Tennyson's affections. Catherine herself married Drummond Rawnsley (they were the parents of H.D. Rawnsley, an early member of The Wordsworth Trust, and three years later, in 1895, the founder of the National Trust). Thus it was that the Rawnsleys knew both the bride and the bridegroom over the thirteen years of their relationship before marriage.

My dear Catherine

I have made up my mind to marry in about a month. I have much to do & to settle in the meantime. Pray keep this thing secret. I do not mean even my own family to know.
You gave me a cold shake of the hand when I came away. You should have given me a warm one.

Ever yours
AT

On 1 April 1850 Emily sent a note to Tennyson by way of Catherine Rawnsley:

I thought I would write my note before the others came. Here it is, no beginning nor end, not a note at all a sort of label only. 'Katie told me the poems might be kept until Saturday. I hope I shall not have occassioned any inconvenience to a limit of time; but if I have, I must be forgiven, for I cannot willingly part from what is so precious. The thanks I would say for them and for the faith in me which has trusted them to me must be thought for me, I cannot write them "I have read the poems through and through and through and to me they were and they are ever more and more a spirit monument grand and beautiful, in whose presence I feel admiration and delight, not unmixed with awe. The happiest possible end to this labour of love! But think not its fruits shall so soon perish, for they are life in life, and they shall live, and as the years go on be only the more fully known and loved and reverenced for what they are.["]

So says a true seer. Can anyone guess the name of this seer? After such big words shall I put anything about my own little I? - that I am the happier for having seen these poems and that I shall hope be the better too?[']

The seer to whom Emily refers was Charles Kingsley. The poems are the songs from *The Princess* sent to her by Tennyson.

**152**
**Marriage Licence of Alfred Tennyson and Emily Sarah Sellwood**
15 May 1850
Lincolnshire County Council:
Tennyson Research Centre, Lincoln

Emily writes in her memoir of the marriage:

Shiplake was a delightful parsonage with a terrace garden down to the Thames on whose banks the Snow Flake grew: The grounds were close to the churchyard. These beautifully ivied with fine windows and once stained. The wedding was of the quietest, which made your Father say it was the nicest wedding he had ever been at, the cake did not arrive in time, nor the dress, the white gloves had disappeared in the depths of a carpet bag. However, things were managed and at all events I had real orange flowers as well as conventional. Only my own Father & Cecilia & Edmund Lushington & Charles Weld & Mr Philipson were there and my bridesmaids were my pretty small cousins now Mary Chaplin & Margaret Arden. We went after breakfast to Pangbourne, next day to western Supermare on our way to Clevedon. It seemed a kind of consecration to go there.

**153**
**Lady Elton**
Sketch of the south front of Clevedon Court
1824
Photograph of drawing
Lady Elton Collection

**154**
**Mary Smirke**
St. Andrew's Church
c.1850
Watercolour 23 x 34 cms
Lady Elton Collection

Clevedon Court was Arthur Hallam's ancestral home, and St. Andrew's Church his resting place. It was probably Tennyson's first visit to Hallam's tomb, and it was made at Emily's request.

**155**
**J.M.W. Turner (1775-1851)**
*Coniston Water with Tent Lodge*
1818
Watercolour and bodycolour on grey paper
50.1 x 66 cms
Fitzwilliam Museum

The Tennysons spent part of their honeymoon at Tent Lodge, as the guests of Mr and Mrs James Marshall. Whilst there they were visited by, among others, Matthew Arnold, Thomas Woolner and Thomas Carlyle. The house derives its name from the tent erected earlier on the spot by the writer Elizabeth Smith in her fight against tuberculosis.

**156**
**Emily, Lady Tennyson (1813-1896)**
Portrait by George Frederic Watts
1865
Oil on canvas 60 x 49 cms
Lincolnshire County Council:
Tennyson Research Centre, Lincoln

**157**
**Emily, Lady Tennyson**
By Thomas Woolner
1859
Painted plaster D 23 cms
Private Collection

**158**
**Emily, Lady Tennyson**
Portrait by unknown artist
c.1870
Photograph: positive image 23.8 x 18.6 cms
Lincolnshire County Council:
Tennyson Research Centre, Lincoln

Tennyson's marriage was very happy and successful. Emily answered Tennyson's letters, managed his household, and encouraged him to write poetry. According to some of Tennyson's early friends, however, she managed him rather too well, and obscured his individual genius.

**159**
**Alfred Lord Tennyson and Emily Tennyson**
Two portraits by W. Jeffrey
c.1870
Photograph 8 x 6.5 cms
Lincolnshire County Council:
Tennyson Research Centre, Lincoln

The force and originality of Julia Margaret Cameron's portraiture is seen when set against the more conventional carte de visite images that proliferated at the time.

## Family

**160**
**Hallam and Lionel Tennyson**
Portrait by G.F. Watts
1865
Oil on canvas 65.5 x 51.5 cms
Lincolnshire County Council:
Tennyson Research Centre, Lincoln

Hallam became Tennyson's close companion and full-time secretary after his wife Emily's sudden collapse in health in 1874. Lionel, less conventional than his brother died in 1886, aged only 32.

Cat. 160

**161**
**Hallam Tennyson (1852-1928)**
Portrait by Charles Lutwidge Dodgson ('Lewis Carroll')
1857
Photograph: albumen print 12.5 x 9.5 cms
By Courtesy of the National Portrait Gallery, London

Dodgson and the Tennyson family were friends for some years, until a *froideur* developed over a trivial matter in 1868.

**162**
**Unidentified figure with Hallam and Lionel**
Portrait by unknown artist
No date
Photograph 15 x 11.3 cms
Lincolnshire County Council:
Tennyson Research Centre, Lincoln

**163**
**Alfred Lord Tennyson with Hallam and Lionel**
Portrait by O.G. Rejlander
*c.*1862
Photograph 31 x 25.5 cms
Lincolnshire County Council:
Tennyson Research Centre, Lincoln

**164**
**Alfred Lord Tennyson with his wife and sons**
Portrait by O.G. Rejlander
1863
Photograph 15 x 5.7 cms
Lincolnshire County Council:
Tennyson Research Centre, Lincoln

The Swedish photographer Oscar Gustav Rejlander (1813-75) visited the Tennysons in April and May of 1863. Emily Tennyson writes in her journal for 1 May: 'Meanwhile Rejlander, the Swedish photographer, has been making photographs of some of us. Lionel's very fine, A.'s profile good. . . . The boys like his Norse tales.'

## The Allinghams

**165**
**William Allingham (1824-89)**
Portrait by Arthur Hughes
No date
Pen and ink with pencil 16 x 12.5 cms
Whitworth Art Gallery, Manchester

William Allingham first met Tennyson in 1851, and quickly became a disciple and friend. His diary is the most lively and informative account of Tennyson's day-to-day existence at his home on the Isle of Wight. In 1874 he married the noted watercolourist, Helen Paterson.

**166**
**Alfred Lord Tennyson**
Portrait by William Allingham
18 October 1880
Pencil 11.5 x 9.5 cms
Mr Roy Davids Collection

**167**
**Emily, Lady Tennyson**
Portrait by Helen Allingham
No date
Watercolour 19.7 x 17.8 cms
Lincolnshire County Council:
Tennyson Research Centre, Lincoln

**168**
**Helen Allingham (1848-1926)**
Old Don
No date
Watercolour 9.5 x 15 cms
Lincolnshire County Council:
Tennyson Research Centre, Lincoln

Tennyson had a love of big dogs, and owned several, including a Siberian wolfhound, Karenina.

Cat. 164

## The Lushingtons:

**169**
**Cecilia Lushington, née Tennyson (1817-1909)**
Portrait by Thomas Rodger
No date
Photograph 10 x 6.3 cms
Lincolnshire County Council:
Tennyson Research Centre, Lincoln

**170**
**Edmund Lushington (1811-93)**
Portrait by unknown artist
1876
Photograph 9.5 x 14.2 cms
Trinity College, Cambridge

In 1842, Cecilia, Tennyson's youngest sister, married Edmund Lushington, Professor of Greek at Glasgow University. Tennyson frequently stayed at the Lushingtons' home, Park House near Maidstone. It was Cecilia's marriage that he drew on for the close of *In Memoriam*:

But now set out: the noon is near,
    And I must give away the bride;
    She fears not, or with thee beside
And me behind her, will not fear.

For I that danced her on my knee,
    That watched her on my nurse's arm,
    That shielded all her life from harm
At last must part with her to thee;

Now waiting to be made a wife,
    Her feet, my darling, on the dead;
    Their pensive tablets round her head,
And the most living words of life

Breathed in her ear. The ring is on,
    The 'wilt thou' answered, and again
    The 'wilt thou' asked, till out of twain
Her sweet 'I will' has made you one.

Cat. 163

# 10. The Royal Family

## Prince Albert and Queen Victoria:

Tennyson enjoyed a friendly relationship with the Royal Family. Prince Albert was an admirer of his poetry, and was largely responsible for Tennyson's obtaining the Laureateship. Queen Victoria, in her turn, derived great solace from *In Memoriam* after her husband's death. At one meeting she answered Tennyson's questions with passages from the poem. 'I thought that very pretty', said Tennyson, 'to quote my own words in answer to me.'[37]

### 171
**Prince Albert (1819-1861)**
Portrait by Franz Xaver Winterhalter
1855
Watercolour 38 x 26 cms
Her Majesty the Queen,
Windsor Castle, Royal Library

### 172
**Queen Victoria (1819-1901)**
Portrait by Franz Xaver Winterhalter
1855
Watercolour 38 x 26 cms
Her Majesty the Queen,
Windsor Castle, Royal Library

### 173
**Prince Albert**
Letter to Alfred Lord Tennyson
17 May 1860
Lincolnshire County Council:
Tennyson Research Centre, Lincoln

My dear Mr Tennyson

Will you forgive me if I intrude upon your leisure with a request which I have thought for some little time of making; viz: that you would be good enough to write your name in the accompanying volume of your "Idylls of the King". You would thus add a peculiar value to the book containing those beautiful songs, from the perusal of which I derive the greatest enjoyment. They quite rekindle the feeling with which the legend of King Arthur must have inspired the Chivalry of old, whilst the graceful form in which they are presented blends these feelings with the softer tone of our present age.

Believe me always yours truly Albert.

### 174
**Edward Walford (1823-97)**
*Life of the Prince Consort*
London: Routledge, Warne & Routledge, 1862
Her Majesty the Queen,
Windsor Castle, Royal Library

On the flyleaf is a passage from Tennyson's dedication of the second edition of *Idylls of the King* to Prince Albert. Opposite is a translation of this into Greek by Walford.

### 175
**Alfred Lord Tennyson**
Letter to Queen Victoria
22 September 1883
Lincolnshire County Council:
Tennyson Research Centre, Lincoln

Madam

Our cruize was so unpremeditated as to direction that my wife could not forward your Majesty's letters to me, but could only place it in my hand first after my arrival at home yesterday evening.

I need not say that I have great pleasure in learning that the quotations suggested by me have been approved by your Majesty & that the accompanying lines have been considered applicable. I feared that they were too elliptical.

The sight of the Princess of Wales in the midst of her own family, all of whom seem so royally simple & kindly was, I think, the pleasantest thing that occurred in our whole voyage delighted as it was; for the longer I live the more I value kindness & simplicity among the sons & daughters of men.

Believe me, Madam
Your Majesty's loyal & affectionate Sert
A Tennyson

### 176
**Queen Victoria**
Letter to Alfred Lord Tennyson
25 April 1886
Lincolnshire County Council:
Tennyson Research Centre, Lincoln

The Queen expresses her condolences for the death of Tennyson's younger son, Lionel.

I wish I could express in words how *deeply* & truly I feel for you in this hour of heavy affliction!

You, who have written such words of comfort for others will I am sure feel the comfort of them again in yourself. But it is *terrible* to lose ones grown up Children, when one is no longer young oneself - & to see as I have done - & as you will do now - The sore striken young Widow of one's beloved son! I will not weary you or intrude on your grief - by words of Consolation, which in fact - *can* offer none! But I may from the depth of a heart which has suffered cruely - & lost almost all it cared for & loved best - I *feel* for you, I know what you & your dear Wife are suffering.

And I pray hard to support you.

Pray let your Son Hallam write me a few words by this messenger who takes this over to say how you & Lady Tennyson are.

My Beatrice grieves deeply for her former Playmate poor dear Eleanor - & is very anxious to hear how she is.
Ever yours
afftely
VRI.
I am very grateful for your kind letter.

### 177

**Programme for a performance of Tableaux Vivants**
Osborne, 8 and 10 January 1891
Her Majesty the Queen,
Windsor Castle, Royal Library

### 178

**Alfred Lord Tennyson**
Letter to Queen Victoria
11 February 1891
Her Majesty the Queen,
Windsor Castle, Royal Archives

Tennyson thanks the Queen for photographs of the tableaux at Osborne:

Madam
I am very grateful for your Majesty's kind letter, & for the photograph of the Tableaux.
That of Elaine in the boat seems beautiful, & Arthur's Court with the splendid colouring & old armour must have been very effective.
May I be allowed to add how much my son & his wife felt the kindness of their reception at Osborne & how much they enjoyed the Plays? I am glad to hear from them that Your Majesty is looking so well.
With the loyal devotion of my wife & myself
I am Y$^r$ Majesty's
ever affect$^{te}$ servant
Tennyson

The programme of *tableaux vivants* shows how Queen Victoria's children and grandchildren acted in choreographed (and wordless) scenes and episodes from Tennyson's works. The Royal children were not the only ones to enjoy this activity. Tennyson's influence can be detected years later in distant Prince Edward Isle. In L.M. Montgomery's *Anne of Green Gables*, one of Anne's particular pleasures was to enact such scenes with her friends:

It was Anne's idea that they dramatise Elaine. They had studied Tennyson's poem in school the preceding winter, the Superintendent of Education having prescribed it in the English course for the Prince Edward Island Schools. They had analysed and parsed it and torn it to pieces in general until it was a wonder there was any meaning at all left in it for them, but at least the fair lily maid and Lancelot and Guinevere and King Arthur had become very real people to them, and Anne was devoured by secret regret that she had not been born in Camelot.

Those days, she said, were so much more romantic than the present.

### 179

**Alfred Lord Tennyson**
Telegram to Queen Victoria
6 August 1891
Her Majesty the Queen,
Windsor Castle, Royal Archives

Tennyson thanks the Queen for her birthday message, and reciprocates:

I beg to offer my most affectionate gratitudes for Your Majesty's gracious message and our best wishes for the birthdays.
Tennyson

## The Laureateship

Tennyson took his duties as Laureate seriously, but disliked writing to order. That he could do so, and successfully, was due to an inbuilt patriotism and a natural sympathy with the Queen: 'writing to order is what I hate. They think a poet can write poems to order as a bootmaker makes boots. For the Queen I am obliged to do it, but she has been very kind and has only asked me once or twice. They call the "Ode on the Duke of Wellington" to Laureate Ode; nothing of the kind! It was written from genuine admiration of the man.'[38]

### 180

**Prince Albert**
Letter to Lord John Russell
8 September 1850
Her Majesty the Queen,
Windsor Castle, Royal Archives

Prince Albert asks the Prime Minister for recommendations for office of Poet Laureate:

The office of Poet Laureate is still vacant. Can you recommend a fit person for it. M$^r$ Rogers declined last summer. If the office is left unfilled we shall be accused of keeping it so in order to save the salary for the Privy Purse.

### 181

**Lord John Russell (1792-1878)**
Letter to Queen Victoria
9 September 1850
Her Majesty the Queen,
Windsor Castle, Royal Archives

Russell's reply mentions Tennyson's name among his recommendations for Poet Laureate. He writes:

Lord John Russell has had the honour of receiving at

Taymouth a letter from the Prince - He agrees that the office of Poet Laureate ought to be filled up. There are 3 or 4 authors of nearly equal merit such as Henry Taylor, Sheridan Knowles, Professor Wilson and Mr Tennyson.

## 182
**Queen Victoria**
Letter to Lord John Russell
16 September 1850
Her Majesty the Queen,
Windsor Castle, Royal Archives

The letter concludes:

The Queen forgot to mention that we think M^r Tennyson would be the fittest person to be Poet Laureate

## 183
**Royal Warrant declaring Tennyson Poet Laureate**
19 November 1850
Lincolnshire County Council:
Tennyson Research Centre, Lincoln

## 184
**James Henry Leigh Hunt (1784-1859)**
Letter to Alfred Lord Tennyson
25 November 1850
Lincolnshire County Council:
Tennyson Research Centre, Lincoln

A failed rival, the one-time friend of Byron, Shelley and Keats, congratulates Tennyson on becoming Poet Laureate:

My dear Alfred Tennyson

Before I say anything else, let me congratulate you on an appointment, which I trust will just happily piece out some defect of your purse, and to which I am sure you will do abundance of honour & glory. I never, thank God, wished anything but happiness to persons more fortunate than myself, however I might have looked to see the ball rolling to my own side; but in the present instance I do not need the comfort of this reflection; for though I once considered my chance of the Laureate ship not impossible, I have for some time passed ceased to think it even possible; especially since my avowal of those opinions in Religion & which were already attributed to me, and which the confessional nature of an Autobiography seemed to render it incumbent on me to acknowledge - May you live to sing congratulations to good Queen Victoria, long after I can hear them with mortal ears.

Pray do not think it indelicate as well as an importunate (or indeed either) if I follow up this benediction with another word on what I wrote to you about last. Carlyle, the other day, encouraged me to send to you again, at the eleventh hour, in case something might still possible turn up among your papers, even if it were but one epigram or a thought in a distich, or the least possible fragment of something larger to show that

you wished me well. He will contribute some interesting matter to the first number, and I hope, to others; and in order to show you how you need not be afraid of at all "committing" yourself either on his account or mine the Address at the commencement of the formal will expressly state that no correspondent of it will be answerable for the opinions of any other, and you will find a mention of "Downing Street" in the same number (for I continue "The Town") in which all the honour will be paid by me to Lord John. I am quite aware, however that there are almost always circumstances connected with questions of delicacy (if this be one) of which no one can be a thorough judge but the party principally concerned - and as to epigrams & distichs, I myself know what it is to be wanting, at some such moment, even in those: so pray believe, that whatever be your ability or non-ability on the occasion, the best of it will be thought of it on my part. Also, my dear Tennyson, think, please, the best of me and this my second, & I must own, somewhat blushing application!

Ever truly yours. Leigh Hunt

## 185
**Alfred Lord Tennyson**
*Ode on the Death of the Duke of Wellington*
1852
Holograph manuscript
Trinity College, Cambridge

Tennyson's first publication as Poet Laureate.

Cat. 186

**186**

**Arthur Wellesley, Duke of Wellington (1769-1852)**
George Richmond
1846
Pen and ink 18.3 x 11.1 cms
Spedding Collection

Although Tennyson looked towards Wellington as something of a hero, he had no desire to make his acquaintance. When Milnes offered to introduce the Duke to him in London he refused with the words 'What the devil do you suppose the Duke wants to see me for?'[39]

**187**

**Alfred Lord Tennyson**
Poem composed in honour of the marriage of Grand Duchess Marie Alexandrovna
1874
Holograph manuscript
Her Majesty the Queen,
Windsor Castle, Royal Archives

The Grand Duchess was the daughter of the Russian Tsar against whom England fought in the Crimea.

**188**

**Lady Augusta Stanley**
Letter to Queen Victoria
4 March 1874
Her Majesty the Queen, Windsor Castle, Royal Archives

The letter, enclosing Tennyson's poem to the Grand Duchess Marie Alexandrovna, begins:

Madam,

I have the inexpressible pleasure & honour of forwarding to Your Majesty lines which will I am sure give Your Majesty pleasure & call forth Your Majesty's Admiration - Tennyson did not feel, when we saw him before Xmas, that he could put his thoughts into a harmonious shape - and Your Majesty knows how impatient of all considerations but the breathings of the Gods, his muse is, at least how very little at his own command or under his own control.

Our surprise and delight were equal when we heard three days ago that he had felt able to write and we have been waiting impatiently for the arrival of the M.S. which, as it turns out, had been addressed to me and mislaid for two days owing to my being out of the way. - I have kept a copy will You Majesty sanction my sending it to the Empress I think it could not but please Her? - I daresay Your Majesty will allow M^r Tennyson to know, if, as I feel sure, Your Majesty approves And is pleased to accept the Poem. - . . . .

# The Royal Library

Queen Victoria and especially Prince Albert were very keen to add to the great Royal Library housed at Windsor Castle, and Tennyson, who usually hated to sign his works, was always prompt in sending them an autographed, finely bound edition of his latest work.

**189**

**Alfred Lord Tennyson**
Letter to an unknown member of the Royal Household
8 June 1857
Her Majesty the Queen,
Windsor Castle, Royal Archives

Attached to *Poems*, 1857.

My Lord

Will you do me the kindness to present the accompanying volume of illustrated Poems to the Queen & to request Her Majesty's gracious acceptance of it?

I am Your Lordships
Ob^t. Ser^t.
A Tennyson

**190**

**Alfred Lord Tennyson**
*Idylls of the King*
London: Moxon & Co., 1859
Her Majesty the Queen,
Windsor Castle, Royal Library

Inscribed: 'Tennyson May 19th 1860'

**191**

**Alfred Lord Tennyson**
*Idylls of the King*
London: Moxon & Co., 1862
Her Majesty the Queen,
Windsor Castle, Royal Library

Containing a letter to the Hon. Sir Charles Phipps, Keeper of the Privy Purse, explaining that the new edition begins with a dedication to the memory of the late Prince Consort.

**192**

**J. Dixon Piper**
Letter to Sir Charles Phipps
18 November 1863
Her Majesty the Queen,
Windsor Castle, Royal Archives

Sir,

About the middle of last year I sent a photograph of Tennyson's "In Memoriam" directed to you at Balmoral, somehow it missed you, and I forwarded another copy to you at Buckingham Palace. I have heard since through the honourable Lady Middleton that Her Majesty the Queen has seen it & expressed approval of it, I had hoped I might have received other orders for, but as so long time has elapsed I suppose I shall not now

I beg now to respectfully hand you the account of them.

> I have the honour to be
> Sir,
> Your obedient servant
> J. Dixon Piper

## 193
**Alfred Lord Tennyson**
*Elaine*: Illustrated by Gustave Doré
London: Moxon & Co., 1867
Her Majesty the Queen,
Windsor Castle, Royal Library

## 194
**Edward Moxon (1801-1858)**
Bill for Tennyson volumes for a Christmas present
20 November 1867
Her Majesty the Queen,
Windsor Castle, Royal Archives

## 195
**Alfred Lord Tennyson**
*The Cup and the Falcon*
London: Macmillan & Co., 1884
Her Majesty the Queen,
Windsor Castle, Royal Library

Inscribed: 'The Queen from her loyal servant Tennyson March 3ᵈ 1884 Alfred Lord Tennyson'

## 196
**Alfred Lord Tennyson**
*Tiresias and Other Poems*
London: Macmillan & Co., 1885
Her Majesty the Queen,
Windsor Castle, Royal Library

Inscribed: 'The Queen from Tennyson. Decr 10th 1885'

## 197
**Alfred Lord Tennyson**
*Tiresias and Other Poems*
London: Macmillan & Co., 1885
Her Majesty the Queen,
Windsor Castle, Royal Library

Inscribed: 'HRH The Princess of Wales from Tennyson Decr 10th 1885'

## 198
**Alfred Lord Tennyson**
*Poems: Illustrated by Edward Lear*
London: Boussod, Valadon & Co., 1889

Her Majesty the Queen,
Windsor Castle, Royal Library

Inscribed: 'The Queen from Her loyal & devoted servant Tennyson'

## 199
*The Book of Common Prayer*
Oxford: University Press, [1890]
Her Majesty the Queen,
Windsor Castle, Royal Library

Presented to Queen Victoria on the fiftieth anniversary of her wedding by her surviving children. The watercolour frontispiece (by the Librarian, Richard Holmes) incorporates lines by Tennyson:

Remembering Him who waits thee far away,
And with thee, Mother, taught us first to pray,
Accept on this your golden bridal day,
      The Book of Prayer.

## 200
**Alfred Lord Tennyson**
*The Death of Oenone, Akbar's Dream
& Other Poems*
London: Macmillan & Co., 1892
Her Majesty the Queen,
Windsor Castle, Royal Library

Inscribed: 'The Queen from Her Majesty's most devoted servant [Hallam] Tennyson October 1892'

## 201
**Alfred Lord Tennyson**
*The Foresters: Robin Hood & Maid Marian*
London: Macmillan & Co., 1892
Her Majesty the Queen,
Windsor Castle, Royal Library

Inscribed: 'The Queen from Tennyson May 1892'

## 202
**Alfred Lord Tennyson**
*The Foresters: Robin Hood & Maid Marian*
London: Macmillan & Co., 1892
Her Majesty the Queen,
Windsor Castle, Royal Library

Inscribed: 'The Princess of Wales from Tennyson May 1892'

## 203
**Alfred Lord Tennyson**
*Seven Poems and Two Translations*
London: Doves Press, No 1 The Terrace, Hammersmith, 1902
Her Majesty the Queen,
Windsor Castle, Royal Library

## Royal Artists

From the seventeenth century most royal princes and princesses received drawing and painting lessons as part of their general education. Queen Victoria encouraged her daughters, the Princess Royal and Princess Alice, to draw scenes from Tennyson's Arthurian poems, which earlier had been so greatly admired by Prince Albert, and in April 1852 Edward Henry Corbould was appointed royal drawing master. His style and palette can be clearly seen in the work of his enthusiastic and accomplished pupils.

### 204

**Edward Henry Corbould (1815-1905)**
*King Arthur's charge to the nuns respecting Guinevere*
No date
Watercolour 56 x 44 cms
Her Majesty the Queen,
Windsor Castle, Royal Library

And lo, he sat on horseback at the door!
And near him the sad nuns with each a light
Stood, and he gave them charge about the Queen,
To guard and foster her for evermore.
And while he spake to these his helm was lowered,
To which for crest the golden dragon clung
Of Britain. . .
> (*Guinevere*, 585-591)

### 205

**Edward Henry Corbould (1815-1905)**
*Elaine*
Signed and dated 1867
Watercolour with bodycolour, gum arabic and heightened with white
59.7 x 84.4 cms
Jeremy Maas Galleries

### 206

**Victoria, Princess Royal (1840-1901)**
*Guinevere being comforted by a nun*
No date
Watercolour
43 x 28 cms
Her Majesty the Queen,
Windsor Castle, Royal Library

And when she came to Almesbury she spoke
There to the nuns, and said, 'Mine enemies
Pursue me, but, O peaceful Sisterhood,
Receive, and yield me sanctuary, nor ask
Her name to whom ye yield it, till her time
To tell you:' and her beauty, grace and power,
Wrought as a charm upon them, and they spared
To ask it.
> (*Guinevere*, 137-144)

### 207

**Victoria, Princess Royal**
*Guinevere begging forgiveness of King Arthur*
No date
Watercolour 34 x 47 cms
Her Majesty the Queen,
Windsor Castle, Royal Library

And while she grovelled at his feet,
She felt the King's breath wander o'er her neck,
And in the darkness o'er her fallen head,
Perceived the waving of his hands that blest.
> (*Guinevere*, 577-580)

### 208

**Princess Alice (1843-78)**
*Scene from Enid (Idylls of the King)*
Signed and dated 26 August 1860
Watercolour 34 x 25 cms
Her Majesty the Queen,
Windsor Castle, Royal Library

### 209

**Princess Alice**
*Scene from Enid (Idylls of the King)*
Signed and dated 26 August 1860
Watercolour 23 x 34 cms
Her Majesty the Queen,
Windsor Castle, Royal Library

. . . so the ruffians growled,
Fearing to lose, and all for a dead man,
Their chance of beauty from the morning raid,
Yet raised and laid him on a litter-bier,
Such as they brought upon their forays out
For those that might be wounded; laid him on it
All in the hollow of his shield, and took
And bore him to the naked hall of Doorm,
(His gentle charger following him unled)
And cast him and the bier in which he lay
Down on an oaken settle in the hall'
> (*Geraint and Enid*, 562-572)

### 210

**Princess Alice**
*Scene from Enid (Idylls of the King)*
Signed and dated 26 August 1860
Watercolour 39 x 62 cms
Her Majesty the Queen,
Windsor Castle, Royal Library

So for long hours sat Enid by her lord,
There in the naked hall, propping his head,
And chafing his pale hands, and calling to him.
Till at last he wakened from his swoon,
And found his own dear bride propping his head,
And chafing his faint hands, and calling to him'
> (*Geraint and Enid*, 579-584)

Cat. 209

Cat. 210

Cat. 212

Cat. 207

211
**Princess Alice**
Moonlit scene after battle
No date
Watercolour 30 x 47 cms
Her Majesty the Queen,
Windsor Castle, Royal Library

212
**Princess Alice (1843-78)**
The Lady of Shalott
Signed and dated 24 May 1862
Watercolour 23 x 31 cms
Her Majesty the Queen,
Windsor Castle, Royal Library

Lying, robed in snowy white
That loosely flew to left and right
The leaves upon her falling light
Through the noises of the night
She floated down to Camelot:
And as the boat-head wound along
The willowy hills and fields among,
They heard her singing her last song,
The Lady of Shalott.

(*The Lady of Shalott*, 136-144)

213
**Victoria, Princess Royal (1840-1901)**
Scene from Romeo and Juliet
Signed and dated 26 August 1861
Watercolour 63 x 45 cms
Her Majesty the Queen,
Windsor Castle, Royal Library

*Romeo and Juliet* was a favourite subject with the Princesses. The Princess Royal was to remind the Queen of another watercolour on the same subject 'which dear Papa helped me with so kindly, - do you remember - one day when you came back from the Drawing room Papa washed out the sky with a sponge?'[40]

"Maud"
1855

Cat. 214

# 11. 'Maud'

*Maud*, like *In Memoriam*, is a collection of short poems, but here in a variety of metrical forms, and expressing a variety of moods. The drama, the monodrama, as Tennyson called the poem (since a single consciousness is dominant), lies in the juxtaposition, even the clash of poems and moods. Action - a duel or a death - takes place between poems, for Tennyson's power, as ever, is in evoking states of mind: despair, lack of confidence, yearning, hope, ecstacy, desire, or pain so fierce that even the expectation of death could not relieve the anguish. Death for the hero of *Maud* would not be the sweet sleep it might have seemed for that dreamless head of *In Memoriam*, but the torment of being awake in a shallow grave,

> My heart is a handful of dust,
> And the wheels go over my head.

The landscape of the poem, like the fluctuating mind, moves mainly back and forth from dismal hollow, to the little wood, to the garden of night-scented flowers where the dawn deepens from faint light to a daffodil sky, as the hero feels momentarily such power in his love that were Maud to come 'My dust would hear her and beat, / Had I lain for a century dead'.

Tennyson's imagination, despite this narrow geography, moves through immense spaces: the dark cedar takes us far back in time to Eden when the tree's 'great forefathers of the thornless garden' were there 'shadowing the snow-limbed Eve'; the 'sad astrology' of the stars with their power to 'burn and brand His nothingness into man' takes us far into a terrible space. The poem has some great moments, and Tennyson surely was right to be excited about it.

Indeed, he regarded *Maud* as his finest achievement. In it he finally managed to face his early life, and exorcise his fears of 'the black blood of the Tennysons'. He described the poem as 'a little *Hamlet*, the history of a morbid, poetic soul, under the blighting influence of a restlessly speculative age. He is the heir of madness, an egoist with the makings of a cynic, raised to a pure and holy love which elevates his whole nature'[41].

Tennyson had a profound need to read *Maud* at every available opportunity, and there are many descriptions of him doing so. He was, according to Jane Carlyle, 'as sensitive to criticisms as if they were imputations on his honour'. Elizabeth Browning wrote of a reading Tennyson made at her husband's home in 1855:

If I had a heart to spare, certainly he would have won mine. He is captivating with his frankness, confidingness and unexampled naïveté. Think of his stopping in

"Maud" every now and then "There's a wonderful touch! That's very tender! How beautiful that is!" Yes, it was wonderful, tender and beautiful, and he read exquisitely in a voice like an organ, rather music than speech.[42]

*Maud* was published in 1855, during the Crimean War, and Tennyson felt called upon to defend the patriotic fervour of the poem's conclusion. In a letter to Archer Gurney on 6 December 1855 he wrote: 'How could you or anyone suppose that if I had had to speak in my own person my own opinion of this war or war generally I should have spoken with so little moderation. The whole was intended to be a new form of dramatic composition. I took a man constitutionally diseased and dipt him into the circumstances of the time and took him out on fire.'

214
**Dante Gabriel Rossetti (1828-1822)**
Tennyson reading 'Maud'
1855
Watercolour 21 x 15 cms
Birmingham Museums and Art Gallery

Rossetti made the drawing without Tennyson's knowledge, and described the reading, done at Robert Browning's, as follows: 'whilst the fiery passages were delivered with a voice and vehemence which he alone of living men can compass, the softer passages and the songs made the tears course down his cheeks.'[43] Another copy exists in the United States.

215
**Alfred Lord Tennyson**
'Come into the garden Maud'
No date
Holograph manuscript
Trinity College, Cambridge

A recording survives, made by Thomas Edison in 1890, of Tennyson reading the final stanza of this part of the poem. The composer C.V. Stanford recalled:

His manner of reading poetry has often been described. It was a chant rather than a declamation. A voice of deep and penetrating power, varied only by alteration of note and by intensity of quality. The notes were few, and he rarely read on more than two, except at the cadence of a passage, when the voice would slightly fall. He often accompanied his reading by gentle rippling gestures with his fingers. . . . "Maud" he also read with a most extraordinary warmth and charm, particularly the climax to "Come into the garden"[44]

two

Into the ~~valley~~ of Death
　Rode the six hundred,
For up came an order, which
　Some one had blunder'd;
'Forward the light Brigade!'
'Take the guns' Nolan said;
Into the ~~valley~~ two of Death
Rode the six hundred.

Honour the
'~~Forward~~ the light Brigade'!
Hearts that were not
~~No man was there~~ dismay'd,
Not tho' the soldier knew
　Some one had blunder'd:

Theirs not to make reply,
Theirs not to reason why,
Theirs but to do ~~and~~ die,
~~Into the valley of Death~~　So they rode onward
~~Rode the six hundred.~~

Cannon to right of them
Cannon to left of them
Cannon in front of them
　Volley'd and thunder'd

Half a league half a league
　Half a league onward
All in
Attack the valley of death
Rode the six hundred.

Cat. 216

# 12. The Charge of the Light Brigade

Tennyson's best-known poem, *The Charge of the Light Brigade*, is here accompanied by early photographs of the Crimea by Roger Fenton (1819-1869), one of Britain's great pioneer photographers.

The Crimean War (1854-6) grew out of French and British alarm at a vast and aggressive Russian empire. As the first major conflict to involve Britain since Waterloo (Lord Raglan, the Commander-in-Chief, still called *the* enemy "the French"), it was greeted with great popular approval at home. But the situation quickly worsened; the press was alive with graphic descriptions of disease and physical hardship (more people died of cholera than in battle), and there were constant accusations of military incompetence. It was to restore public confidence in a so far unsuccessful war that Fenton went to the Crimea in 1855. He left after only six months, with cholera and 360 photographs.

The photographs avoid both the horrors of war and the rhetoric of propaganda. They are instead revealingly matter-of-fact. In the public eye, the hero of the Crimea was not, as in previous campaigns, the aristocratic officer, but the common soldier - more Trooper Pearson than Lord Raglan.

216
**Alfred Lord Tennyson**
*Charge of the Light Brigade*
1854
Holograph manuscript
Lincolnshire County Council:
Tennyson Research Centre, Lincoln

217
**Alfred Lord Tennyson**
*The Charge of the Light Brigade*
Published in *The Examiner*, 9 December 1854
Spedding Collection

**The Charge of the Light Brigade**

Half a league, half a league,
  Half a league onward,
All in the valley of Death
  Rode the six hundred.

Into the valley of Death
  Rode the six hundred,
For up came an order which
  Some one had blunder'd.
'Forward, the Light Brigade!
'Take the guns!' Nolan said:
Into the valley of Death
  Rode the six hundred.

'Forward, the Light Brigade!'
  No man was there dismay'd,
Not tho' the soldier knew
  Some one had blunder'd:
Theirs not to make reply,
Theirs not to reason why,
Theirs but to do and die:
Into the valley of Death
  Rode the six hundred.

Cannon to right of them,
Cannon to left of them,
Cannon in front of them
  Volley'd and thunder'd;
Stormed at with shot and shell,
Boldly they rode and well,
Into the jaws of Death,
Into the mouth of Hell
  Rode the six hundred.

Flash'd all their sabres bare,
Flash'd all at once in air
Sabring the gunners there,
Charging an army, while
  All the world wonder'd:
Plunged in the battery smoke,
With many a desperate stroke
The Russian line they broke;
Then they rode back, but not
  Not the six hundred.

Cannon to right of them,
Cannon to left of them,
Cannon behind them
  Volley'd and thunder'd;
Storm'd at with shot and shell,
While horse and hero fell,
Those that had fought so well
Came from the jaws of Death,
Back from the mouth of Hell,
  All that was left of them,
  Left of six hundred.

What can their glory fade?
O the wild charge they made!
  All the world wonder'd.
Honour the charge they made!
Honour the Light Brigade,
  Noble six hundred!

                              A.T.

218
**Lord Cardigan (1767-1868)**
Sir George Frampton after Maraschetti
Bronze H 61 cms
Lent by Edmund Brudenell Esq.

Lord Cardigan was the first to reach the Russian guns at the Charge of the Light Brigade, and returned home a hero.

**219**
**Sword belonging to Lord Cardigan**
L 91 cms
Lent by Edmund Brudenell Esq.

**220**
**Roll containing over 4,000 signatures presented to Lord Cardigan on his return from the Crimea**
Vellum L 6400 cms
Lent by Edmund Brudenell Esq.

Given 'to express in the strongest terms our admiration of your heroic conduct at Balaclava and your gallant services - of which we as Englishmen and Northamptonshire men are justly proud'.

**221**
**Laporte**
*Lord Cardigan's Engagement with Two Cossacks Behind the Russian Guns*
Oil on canvas 122 x 91 cms
Lent by Edmund Brudenell Esq.

**222**
*'Ronald' with Tents of Army Camp in the background*
Oil on canvas 61 x 45 cms
Lent by Edmund Brudenell Esq.

'Ronald' was Lord Cardigan's horse in the Crimea.

**223**
**Replica of the Balaclava Bugle**
17th/21st Lancers Regimental Museum,
Belvoir Castle, Grantham

A replica of the bugle carried by Trumpet-Major Henry Joy at Balaclava in 1854, holed and dented in imitation of the original.

**224**
**A Uniform of the Crimean Period**
*c.* 1854-5
17th/21st Lancers Regimental Museum,
Belvoir Castle, Grantham

Lance cap, full dress uniform, sword and lance similar to the type used by the 17th Lancers in the Crimea 1854-5.

**225**
**Patriotic Jug**
H 25.4 cms
Lent by Edmund Brudenell Esq.

**226**
**Trooper William Pearson (1826-1909)**
E. Fowler Richards of Penrith
1864

Photograph 56.5 x 42
Courtesy of Eden District Council,
Penrith Museum

Trooper Pearson, of Penrith, was a survivor of the charge of the Light Brigade. Whilst in the Crimea he was nursed by Florence Nightingale and in 1855 he was presented to Queen Victoria.

The left-hand inscription reads: 'Served through the whole of the Crimean War, and was present at Alma, Balaclava, Inkermann, and the Seige of Sebastopol, where he lost his toes from frostbite in the winter of 1854-5. - Had his horse shot under him at Balaclava, and received a slight wound in the forehead, caught a riderless horse of the 8th Hussars, and rode back without further injury.'

## Roger Fenton (1819-1869)

Roger Fenton was the son of a wealthy Lancashire family whose grandfather had built up the fortune and whose father was the first (Whig) member of parliament for Rochdale. He trained in law and in painting. Fenton was to present the photographs to the Queen and to the French Emperor, Louis Napoleon. These were issued to dealers such as Thomas Agnews and Sons. After ten years as a photographer, Fenton gave up an art in which he had been a major figure.

**227**
**Roger Fenton**
*The Valley of the Shadow of Death*
1855
Photograph 25.5 x 35 cms
Her Majesty the Queen,
Windsor Castle, Royal Archives

This name was applied, not to the scene of the Charge of the Light Brigade (which Tennyson calls 'the Valley of Death'), but to one of the five ravines running north-west from the plateau south-east of Sebastopol to the walls of the city. It was so called because shots from the Russian defences at one of the British beseiger's batteries, Chapman's Battery, often overshot and landed in the ravine in question. Another Fenton photograph exists in which there are fewer cannon balls. Obviously cannon were introduced to give the picture a more dramatic and elegiac feel.

**228**
**Roger Fenton**
*Field Marshal Lord Raglan*
1855

Photograph 18.5 x 14 cms
Her Majesty the Queen,
Windsor Castle, Royal Archives

Commander-in-Chief of British forces in the Crimea. His early career was spent serving under the Duke of Wellington, who described him as 'a man who wouldn't tell a lie to save his life'. It was when standing beside Wellington at Waterloo that he lost his right arm. As Commander-in-Chief he was charged with neglect and incompetence by the *Times*, but at his death in 1855 the strength of his character was widely recognised. Three months later *The Leader* commented on this portrait:

There is no spectacle more affecting than the countenance of Lord Raglan. . . . It not only reconciles us to the man, but to our own estimation; teaching us that after all there was no mistake in the respect paid to the character of Lord Raglan. The mistake lay in permitting a noble ambition to indulge itself, where a gentle force ought to have been used in making the aged man accept the repose which his patriotism spurned.[45]

**229**
**Roger Fenton**
*Lord Raglan's Headquarters with Lord Raglan, Marshal Pélissier, Lord Burghersh, Spahi and Aide-de-Camp of Marshal Pélissier*
1855
Photograph 19 x 16.5 cms
Her Majesty the Queen,
Windsor Castle, Royal Archives

Only forty years after Waterloo and the Peninsula War the British and the French found themselves fighting on the same side. Their alliance was not without tension. Raglan, who was present at Waterloo, had the unfortunate habit of referring to the enemy as the French, and Marshal Pélissier once likened the British advance to a stroll in Hyde Park. Nevertheless, he and Raglan shared a mutual respect. On the latter's death, Pélissier praised 'the calm and stoic greatness of his character throughout this rude and memorable campaign.'

Lord Raglan, in the panama hat, is cunningly placed so that his lack of a right arm is not visible.

**230**
**Roger Fenton**
*Photographic Van*
1855
Photograph 18 x 24 cms
Her Majesty the Queen,
Windsor Castle, Royal Archives

Fenton's photographic van, a former wine

merchant's van converted by him into a portable dark room, was later to become a well-known sight in England. In the Crimea, it was often the target of enemy fire, on one occasion losing its roof. This photograph was taken just before Fenton took it down the Valley of the Shadow of Death, in case it didn't survive the journey.

The man on the box is Marcus Sparling, one of his two assistants, who also drove the van and looked after the horses. He was a former corporal in the 4th Light Dragoons.

**231**
**Roger Fenton**
*Officers of the Fourth Light Dragoons*
1855
Photograph 18 x 16 cms
Her Majesty the Queen,
Windsor Castle, Royal Archives

This regiment shared the 3rd (rear) line of the Light Brigade with the 8th Hussars. Several of the officers are wearing beards; beards became fashionable after the Crimean War.

**232**
**Roger Fenton**
*Chasseurs D'Afriques*
1855
Photograph 17.5 x 24 cms
Her Majesty the Queen,
Windsor Castle, Royal Archives

These French colonial troops, which had recently seen service in North Africa, were sent to clear a Russian battery from the lower slopes of the Fedukhine Heights, on the northern side of the Light Brigade's route. The success of the Chasseurs in their skirmish reduced the crossfire through which the Brigade's survivors had to return.

**233**
**Roger Fenton**
*William Russell Esq, The Times Correspondent*
1855
Photograph 18 x 15 cms
Her Majesty the Queen,
Windsor Castle, Royal Archives

W.H. Russell is the first, and perhaps the greatest, of war correspondents. It was largely in reponse to his graphic and critical on-the-spot accounts that Fenton was sent out to the Crimea. According to his son Hallam, Tennyson was inspired to write *The Charge of the Light Brigade* after reading Russell's report of the incident in *The Times*.

234
**Roger Fenton**
*Colonel Shewell, Light Cavalry*
1855
Photograph 18 x 15.5 cms
Her Majesty the Queen,
Windsor Castle, Royal Archives

Frederick George Shewell commanded the 8th
Hussars at the Battle of Balaclava, when it formed
part of the third line in the Charge of the Light
Brigade, and he was one of the two officers who
rallied substantial groups of the survivors, and led
them back to the British lines.

235
**Roger Fenton**
*Five sections of a view of the plains at Balaclava*
1855
Photograph 18 x 24 cms
Her Majesty the Queen,
Windsor Castle, Royal Archives

236
**Roger Fenton**
*Eleven sections of a panoramic view of the plateau
before Sebastopol, beginning at Inkerman*
1855
Photograph 27 x 36 cms
Her Majesty the Queen,
Windsor Castle, Royal Archives

The two panoramas, of Balaclava and the plateau
before Sebastopol, show the scale and detail of the
operation, and the barrenness of the landscape
where it took place. Technically, they suffer from
the constant variation in the atmosphere caused by
heat and humidity, which affected the horizon from
one negative to the next.

237
**Two wax cylinders of the kind used to record
Tennyson's voice and the Balaclava bugle**
Miles Mallinson Collection

Cat. 233

# 13. Illustrated Works, 1857

In 1857 an illustrated edition of Tennyson's poetry was published by Edward Moxon. Among the distinguished list of artists who contributed were Rossetti, Millais, and Holman Hunt. Many of the younger artists were later to take Tennyson's poems as a proper subject for their more ambitious paintings. In his 1855 essay on Thackeray's *The Newcomers* Burne-Jones wrote: 'When shall we learn to read a picture as we do a poem, to find some story from it, some little atom of human interest that may feed our heart within lest the outer influences of the day crush them from good thoughts? When will men look for these things and the artist satisfy them?' He named Tennyson as one of those 'who have led on this most godly crusade against falsehood, doubt and wretched fashion, against hypocrisy and mammon and lack of earnestness'.

The volume was, by Tennyson's standards, only a modest commercial success, but was praised by Ruskin: 'I wanted to congratulate you on the last edition of your poems . . . many of the plates are very noble things'.

Here the process of book illustration can be traced from the initial pencil studies, to the proofs, and finally to the publication itself. The illustrations are taken both from the proofs and the pages.

Cat. 238

**238**
**Edward Moxon (1801-1858)**
Portrait by unknown artist
No date
Oil on canvas 74 x 61 cms
Private Collection

Moxon's entry into the Tennyson circle was through the energies of Arthur Hallam, who contacted him as soon as he heard that Moxon had become the publisher of *The Englishman's Magazine* in July 1831. Moxon, an employee of Longmans, was nevertheless setting up his own publishing concerns - he had the support of Samuel Rogers, who was a banker as well as a poet, and Charles Lamb, who introduced him to Wordsworth and to Southey. Hallam acted as middle-man with the publication of Tennyson's *Poems*, 1833, Moxon already being an admirer.

Moxon was to be Tennyson's publisher till his death in 1857, the year in which his *Illustrated Tennyson* appeared. It was a generous commission to many English artists, several being the Pre-Raphaelites, who thereafter thought of Tennyson's works as one of the natural subjects for their art.

**239**
**Alfred Lord Tennyson**
Illustrated Poems
London: E. Moxon 1857
Lincolnshire County Council:
Tennyson Research Centre, Lincoln

**240**
**William Holman Hunt (1827-1910)**
Study for Ballad of Oriana
1856-7
Pencil on paper 14.6 x 10.8 cms
Birmingham Museums and Art Gallery

**241**
**William Holman Hunt**
Letter to Alfred Lord Tennyson
26 February 1856
Lincolnshire County Council:
Tennyson Research Centre, Lincoln

Tennyson's friendship with artists was full of the tension that always exists between rival poets. Here Hunt delightfully shows the connections between poetry, tobacco, travelling and the nobility, beauty and mystery of nature.

Dear Sir,
Since writing to our friend Woolner last night I received a communication from Hickie Borman & Co Southampton acquainting me of the roll of tobacco sent

**Cat. 246**

MARIANA IN THE SOUTH.

WITH one black shadow at its feet,
    The house thro' all the level shines,
Close-latticed to the brooding heat,
    And silent in its dusty vines :
A faint-blue ridge upon the right,
    An empty river-bed before,

**Cat. 239**

**Cat. 251**

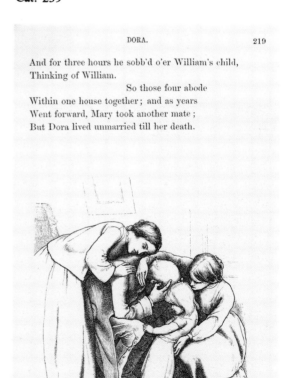

DORA.                                                    219

And for three hours he sobb'd o'er William's child,
Thinking of William.
                        So those four abode
Within one house together; and as years
Went forward, Mary took another mate ;
But Dora lived unmarried till her death.

**Cat. 239**

Cat. 254

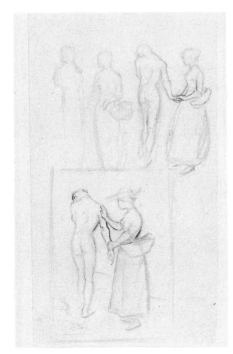

Cat. 261-2

Cat. 274

to their care with my other things from Malta, being at their command - and I have directed them to forward it to you without delay. I trust that it will arrive safely and in good order.

In my solitary journeyings in the East I had the delight of many an hour increased, and the sadness of many others tempered by an ability of appreciating the link between the nobility, beauty, and the mystery of Nature and your manifold renderings of her secrets: in this way in the plain between Libanus and Anti-Libanus after returning to my night-abode from a peaceful ramble in the Temple of Baal, I had your name in my thoughts when the farmer came with some tobacco - that he had grown - to sell, and it occurred to me that this plant which had drawn its life and ripened in that sweet air would not be an inappropriate offering to you if you would do me the honor of accepting it. If you have before smoked tobacco from the neighbourhood you may feel the want of a certain odourous flavour in this, the fragrance peculiar to Latakia and Djebely tobacco brought from Egypt -which is its best market, is imparted to it in being subjected to the fumes of burning oak, or cedar in a close chamber, a process which the tobacco I offer has not been subject to.

With highest regards
I am, Dear Sir, most truly yours
W Holman Hunt

### 242
**Dante Gabriel Rossetti (1828-1882)**
*St Cecilia*
1856-7
Pen and brown ink 9.5 x 8.3 cms
Birmingham Museums and Art Gallery

The design illustrates lines from *The Palace of Art*:

Or in a clear-wall'd city on the sea
Near gilded organ-pipes, her hair
Wound with white roses, slept St. Cecily;
An angel look'd at her.

As Tennyson feared, the artist has departed from the text to expand his own ideas. Rossetti's brother William writes:

Tennyson here speaks of S. Cecilia as sleeping 'while an Angel looked at her'. Rossetti however has chosen to represent the subject from a more special point of view. He supposes Cecilia, while kept as a prisoner for her Christian faith, to be taking the air on the ramparts of the fortress; as she plays on her hand-organ an Angel gives her a kiss, which is the kiss of death. This is what Rossetti meant.[46]

### 243
**Dante Gabriel Rossetti**
*King Arthur and the Weeping Queens*
1856-7
Pen and brown ink 8.3 x 8.9 cms
Birmingham Museums and Art Gallery

An illustration not of the *Idylls of the King*, but of the following lines from *The Palace of Art*:

Or mythic Uther's deeply-wounded son
In some fair space of sloping greens
Lay, dozing in the Vale of Avalon,
And watch'd by weeping queens.

### 244
**Dante Gabriel Rossetti**
*Mariana in the South*
1856-7
Pen and brown ink 9.7 x 9.5 cms
Birmingham Museums and Art Gallery

### 245
**Sir John Everett Millais (1829-1896)**
Study for *Mariana in the South*
*c.*1851
Pencil on paper 10.8 x 5.7 cms
Birmingham Museums and Art Gallery

### 246
**Sir John Everett Millais**
Study for *Mariana in the South*
*c.*1851
Pencil on paper 13.3 x 12.7 cms
Birmingham Museums and Art Gallery

### 247
**Sir John Everett Millais**
Study for *Mariana in the South*
*c.*1851
Pencil on paper 6.4 x 13 cms
Birmingham Museums and Art Gallery

### 248
**Sir John Everett Millais**
Study for *The Talking Oak*
1856-7
Pencil on paper 11.4 x 8.1 cms
Birmingham Museums and Art Gallery

### 249
**Sir John Everett Millais**
Study for *The Talking Oak*
1856-7
Pencil on paper 10.2 x 10.8 cms
Birmingham Museums and Art Gallery

### 250
**John Ruskin (1819-1900)**
Coronet of oak leaves
1856-7
Pencil on paper 3.3 x 7.6 cms
Victoria and Albert Museum

Ruskin here helps Millais with the detail for his illustration of 'The Talking Oak'.

251
**Sir John Everett Millais**
Study for *Dora*
1856-7
Pencil on paper 12.7 x 8.3 cms
Birmingham Museums and Art Gallery

252
**Sir John Everett Millais**
Study for *Dora*
1856-7
Pencil on paper 14 x 18.3 cms
Birmingham Museums and Art Gallery

253
**Sir John Everett Millais**
Study for *Dora*
1856-7
Pencil on paper 13.3 x 11.4 cms
Birmingham Museums and Art Gallery

254
**Sir John Everett Millais**
Two studies for *Dora*
1856-7
Pencil 18.5 x 11.5 cms
Mr Peter Nahum Collection

255
**Sir John Everett Millais**
Design for *Dora*
1856-7
Pencil and wash 13.3 x 15.2 cms
Birmingham Museums and Art Gallery

256
**Sir John Everett Millais**
Study for *The Lord of Burleigh*
1856-7
Pencil on paper 17.8 x 4.6 cms
Birmingham Museums and Art Gallery

257
**Sir John Everett Millais**
Study for *The Miller's Daughter*
1856-7
Pencil on paper 14 x 22.2 cms
Birmingham Museums and Art Gallery

258
**Sir John Everett Millais**
Study for *The Miller's Daughter*

1856-7
Pencil on paper 9.5 x 8 cms
Birmingham Museums and Art Gallery

259
**Sir John Everett Millais**
Study for *The Miller's Daughter*
1856-7
Pencil on paper 17.9 x 12.7 cms
Birmingham Museums and Art Gallery

260
**Sir John Everett Millais**
Study for *The Miller's Daughter*
1856-7
Pencil on paper 13.3 x 11.4 cms
Birmingham Museums and Art Gallery

261
**Sir John Everett Millais**
Study for *The Day-Dream*
1856-7
Pencil on paper 9.5 x 9.5 cms
Birmingham Museums and Art Gallery

262
**Sir John Everett Millais**
Study for *The Day-Dream*
1856-7
Pencil on paper 9.5 x 10.8 cms
Birmingham Museums and Art Gallery

263
**Sir John Everett Millais**
Study for *St Agnes' Eve*
1856-7
Pencil on paper 17.1 x 8 cms
Birmingham Museums and Art Gallery

264
**Sir John Everett Millais**
Study for *St Agnes' Eve*
1856-7
Pencil on paper 14 x 7.6 cms
Birmingham Museums and Art Gallery

265
**Sir John Everett Millais**
Study for *St Agnes' Eve*
1856-7
Pencil on paper 12 x 9.5 cms
Birmingham Museums and Art Gallery

266
**Sir John Everett Millais**

Study for *Edward Gray*
1856-7
Pencil on paper 21.6 x 9.5 cms
Birmingham Museums and Art Gallery

### 267
**Sir John Everett Millais**
Study for *The Sisters*
1856-7
Pencil on paper 12 x 10.5 cms
Birmingham Museums and Art Gallery

### 268
**Sir John Everett Millais**
Study for *The Sisters*
1856-7
Pencil on paper 17.2 x 11.4 cms
Birmingham Museums and Art Gallery

### 269
**Sir John Everett Millais**
Study for *A Dream of Fair Women*
1856-7
Pencil on paper 8.1 x 9.4 cms
Victoria and Albert Museum

### 270
**Sir John Everett Millais**
Study for *A Dream of Fair Women*
1856-7
Pencil on paper 9.4 x 8.1 cms
Victoria and Albert Museum

### 271
**Sir John Everett Millais**
Study for *A Dream of Fair Women*
1856-7
Pencil on paper 10 x 12.5 cms
Victoria and Albert Museum

### 272
**Sir John Everett Millais**
Study for *Mariana in the Moated Grange*
1856-7
Pencil on paper 21.3 x 13.1 cms
Victoria and Albert Museum

### 273
**Sir John Everett Millais**
Letter to Alfred Lord Tennyson
24 August 1854
Lincolnshire County Council:
Tennyson Research Centre, Lincoln

The letter shows Millais' hesitancy about the projected illustrations, his first important commission in engravings. He met Tennyson at Farringford in November that year, but the writer was difficult to please. He insisted that 'the illustrator should always adhere to the words of the poet', and Millais said that Tennyson hated his designs. In all he contributed eighteen of the fifty-four illustrations.

My dear Sir

I am very sorry that I have not been able to pay you a visit before this. I have been painting in the North up to this time and am now at work at this place and intending to stay until it is too unseasonable to sit out of doors. The cold and rain will probably come at the end of next month when I purpose taking the Isle of Wight on my way home if it will be convenient for you to see me there -

I have made many sketches of corn fields for Dora. I hope your boy has not grown too large for the character. Some questions I wish to ask you about the poems I am to illustrate but I will keep them until I see you. The end of next month is the time I shall be disengaged. Do not trouble yourself to write if it is convenient for you to see me then -

Yours very truly
John Everett Millais

### 274
**Alfred Lord Tennyson**
Proofs of first edition of *Illustrated Poems*
Bound notebook
1857
Lincolnshire County Council:
Tennyson Research Centre, Lincoln

**Thomas Woolner** (engr. H. Robinson)
Frontispiece: Tennyson

1. **T. Creswick** (engr. T. Williams)
   Illustration to *Claribel*
2. **J.E. Millais** (engr. Dalziel Brothers)
   Illustration to *Mariana*
3. **William Holman Hunt** (engr. T. Williams)
   Illustration to *Recollections of the Arabian Knights*
4. **William Holman Hunt** (engr. J. Thompson)
   Illustration to *Recollections of the Arabian Knights*
5. **T. Creswick** (engr. W.J. Linton)
   Illustration to *Ode to Memory*
6. **W. Mulready** (engr. J. Thompson)
   Illustration to *The Sea Fairies*
7. **W. Mulready** (engr. J. Thompson)
   Illustration to *The Deserted House*
8. **T. Creswick** (engr. W.J. Linton)
   Illustration to *A Dirge*
9. **William Holman Hunt** (engr. Dalziel Brothers)
   Illustration to *The Ballad of Oriana*
10. **William Holman Hunt** (engr. Dalziel Brothers)
    Illustration to *The Ballad of Oriana*

11. **J.C. Horsley** (engr. J. Thompson)
Illustration to *Circumstance*

12. **J.C. Horsley** (engr. W.J. Linton)
Illustration to *Circumstance*

13. **William Holman Hunt** (engr. J. Thompson)
Illustration to *The Lady of Shalott*

14. **Dante Gabriel Rossetti** (engr. Dalziel Brothers)
Illustration to *The Lady of Shalott*

15. **Dante Gabriel Rossetti** (engr. W.J. Linton)
Illustration to *Mariana in the South*

16. **J.E. Millais** (engr. T. Williams)
Illustration to *The Miller's Daughter*

17. **J.E. Millais** (engr. J. Thompson)
Illustration to *The Miller's Daughter*

18. **Clarkson Stanfield** (engr. W.J. Linton)
Illustration to *Oenone*

19. **J.E. Millais** (engr. Dalziel Brothers)
Illustration to *The Sisters*

20. **Dante Gabriel Rossetti** (engr. Dalziel Brothers)
Illustration to *The Palace of Art*

21. **Dante Gabriel Rossetti** (engr. Dalziel Brothers)
Illustration to *The Palace of Art*

22. **J.C. Horsley** (engr. W.J. Linton)
Illustration to *The May Queen*

23. **J.C. Horsley** (engr. W.J. Linton)
Illustration to *The May Queen: New Year's Eve*

24. **J.C. Horsley** (engr. W.J. Linton)
Illustration to *The May Queen: Conclusion*

25. **Clarkson Stanfield** (engr. W.J. Linton)
Illustration to *The Lotos-Eaters*

26. **J.E. Millais** (engr. W.J. Linton)
Illustration to *A Dream of Fair Women*

27. **J.E. Millais** (engr. Dalziel Brothers)
Illustration to *A Dream of Fair Women*

28. **J.E. Millais** (engr. Dalziel Brothers)
Illustration to *The Death of the Old Year*

29. **W. Mulready** (engr. J. Thompson)
Illustration to *The Goose*

30. **Daniel Maclise** (engr. J. Thompson)
Illustration to *Morte D'Arthur*

31. **Daniel Maclise** (engr. Dalziel Brothers)
Illustration to *Morte D'Arthur*

32. **J.C. Horsley** (engr. J. Thompson)
Illustration to *The Gardener's Daughter*

33. **J.E. Millais** (engr. T. Williams)
Illustration to *Dora*

34. **J.E. Millais** (engr. J. Thompson)
Illustration to *Dora*

35. **Clarkson Stanfield** (engr. W.J. Linton)
Illustration to *Edwin Morris*

36. **J.E. Millais** (engr. J. Thompson)
Illustration to *The Talking Oak*

37. **J.E. Millais** (engr. Dalziel Brothers)
Illustration to *The Talking Oak*

38. **T. Creswick** (engr. W.T. Green)
Illustration to *The Golden Year*

39. **Clarkson Stanfield** (engr. W.T. Green)
Illustration to *Ulysses*

40. **J.E. Millais** (engr. J. Thompson)
Illustration to *Locksley Hall*

41. **J.E. Millais** (engr. Dalziel Brothers)
Illustration to *Locksley Hall*

42. **William Holman Hunt** (engr. Dalziel Brothers)
Illustration to *Godiva*

43. **Dante Gabriel Rossetti** (engr. W.J. Linton)
Illustration to *Sir Galahad*

44. **J.E. Millais** (engr. Dalziel Brothers)
Illustration to *St. Agnes' Eve*

45. **Clarkson Stanfield** (engr. W.J. Linton)
Illustration to *St Agnes' Eve*

46. **J.E. Millais** (engr. W.J. Linton)
Illustration to *The Day-Dream*

47. **J.E. Millais** (engr. C.T. Thompson)
Illustration to *The Day-Dream*

48. **W. Mulready** (engr. J. Thompson)
Illustration to *Will Waterproof's Lyrical Monologue, made at the Cock*

49. **J.E. Millais** (engr. J. Thompson)
Illustration to *Edward Gray*

50. **T. Creswick** (engr. T. Williams)
Illustration to *A Farewell*

51. **J.E. Millais** (engr. Dalziel Brothers)
Illustration to *The Lord of Burleigh*

52. **William Holman Hunt** (engr. T. Williams)
Illustration to *The Beggar Maid*

53. **T. Creswick** (engr. W.T. Green)
Illustration to "Move eastward, happy earth, and leave"

54. **Clarkson Stanfield** (engr. W.T. Green)
Illustration to "Break, break, break"

# 14. Drama

Tennyson turned to drama late in life, but with increasing success. *Queen Mary*, published in 1875 when the poet was 66 years old, was followed by *Harold*, and then *Becket*, his biggest, though posthumous, stage success. This last had a fine cast, which included Ellen Terry and, in the tile role, Henry Irving. Irving's business manager was Bram Stoker, best-known as the author of *Dracula*.

The commercial success of the plays owed a good deal to the popular music of Charles Villiers Stanford.

**275**
**Alfred Lord Tennyson (1809-1892)**
*The Cup. A Tragedy*
1881
Lincolnshire County Council:
Tennyson Research Cenre, Lincoln

**276**
**Programme for *The Cup* and *The Corsican Brothers***
3 January 1881
Lincolnshire County Council:
Tennyson Research Centre, Lincoln

**277**
**Alfred Lord Tennyson**
*Becket*
1875
Holograph manuscript
Lincolnshire County Council:
Tennyson Research Centre, Lincoln

**278**
**Programme for a command performance of *Becket***
Windsor Castle, 18 March 1893
Her Majesty the Queen,
Windsor Castle, Royal Archives

**279**
**Reginald Cleaver**
*Becket* performed before Queen Victoria
1893
Newspaper print 24.4 x 34 cms
Lincolnshire County Council:
Tennyson Research Centre, Lincoln

**280**
**Henry Irving as Becket**
Unknown artist

1893
Photograph 40 x 34 cms
Michael Meredith Collection

This is a publicity picture used for displaying outside the theatre. Irving played Becket in both England and America. He often programmed it back-to-back with his celebrated melodrama, *The Bells*. His last performance was in *Becket*, played at Bradford.

Cat. 280

**281**
**Henry Irving as Becket**
Unknown artist
1893
Photograph with autograph
Postcard
Michael Meredith Collection

**282**
**Volume of Stage Designs for Tennyson's *Becket***
1893
The Garrick Club

283
**Alfred Lord Tennyson**
*Becket - As Arranged for the Stage by Henry Irving, & in the Lyceum Theatre on 6 February 1893*
London: Macmillan 1893
The Garrick Club

**Aubrey Beardsley**
Kate Phillips as Margery
Cartoon 10.6 x 7.5 cms
Victoria and Albert Museum

**Aubrey Beardsley**
Master Leo Byrne as Geoffrey
Cartoon 10.6 x 7.5 cms
Victoria and Albert Museum

284
**Programme for *Becket***
29 April 1905
Michael Meredith Collection

285
**Programme for *The Promise of May***
11 November 1882
Lincolnshire County Council:
Tennyson Research Centre, Lincoln

286
**Programme for *The Falcon***
17 March 1892
Lincolnshire County Council:
Tennyson Research Centre, Lincoln

287
**Programme for *Enoch Arden***
21 June 1869
Lincolnshire County Council:
Tennyson Research Centre, Lincoln

288
**Alfred Lord Tennyson**
*The Falcon*
Garrick Club

Contains information on stage propoerty, cast lists, diagrams of stage movements and watercolours of the stage set.

289
**Bram Stoker**
Letter to Hallam Tennyson
30 April 1881
Lincolnshire County Council:
Tennyson Research Centre, Lincoln

Bram Stoker's correspondence with Tennyson and Hallam Tennyson lasts over ten years, always dealing with payments and contractual matters.

Cat. 290

290
**Charles Villiers Stanford (1852-1924)**
Portrait by unknown artist
1891
Photograph 16.5 x 10.3 cms
Trinity College, Cambridge

**Charles Villiers Stanford**
Portrait by Aubrey Beardsley
10.6 x 7.5 cms
Victoria and Albert Museum

291
**Charles Villiers Stanford**
Letter to Alfred Lord Tennyson
14 March 1876
Lincolnshire County Council:
Tennyson Research Centre, Lincoln

The youthful Stanford writes to Tennyson from Trinity College, Cambridge (where he was a fellow) to explain his difficulties with Mrs Bateman, the Theatre Manager.

My dear Sir,
  Will you allow me to thank you most sincerely for the kind interest you have taken in the music you allowed me to write for Queen Mary, an interest as valued as it is undeserved. Your son tells me he has written to you about the refusal of Mrs Bateman & her conductor to

perform it, which seems scarcely warranted if I am to believe the opinions which valued critics have given me upon the work. There seem to be several reasons alleged, which however do not all coincide.

(1) the conductor's reason is that the score is on too large a scale for his band, & Mrs Bateman says,

(2) that the orchestra must be beneath the stage (as its being in its proper position w$^d$ entail the loss of some 60 stalls) & therefore that the music could not be properly heard and

(3) That she did not commission me to write entr'actes or overture at all, "Music for a play being music while the curtain is up".

In reply to the first I can only say that those to whom I have shown the score have remarked on its being written for a small band.

To the second, I can only question the amount of loss entailed, & at the same [time] point out that the drawback of having the music principally inaudible would effectually prevent any composer from undertaking work for such an object.

To the third, that (1) all the music to plays of importance (viz Egmont, Rosamund, Precina, Midsummer Night's Dream, Tempest, Merchant of Venice &$^c$) contain what she says she did not commission me to write, *overtures & entractes*, and (2) that she herself at my request last June informed me *what the length of the entractes ought to be*.

The writing of music to such an important play as Queen Mary naturally entailed much thought & work, but this was increased by the subsequent difficulty of adapting my music to a band of numerical proportion such as I never expected. Under all these circumstances I very much doubt the advisability of allowing the performance of the music of the songs & short incidental pieces, which she offers still to perform, & which w$^d$ lose mush of their effect by the absence of their musical surroundings & unity. This I feel sure you will understand at once. I may add that all my Cambridge friends are very indignant at the treatment I am threatened with, more especially as the disappointment may lose me the publication of my overture and entr'actes which had been undertaken by a well known firm. I have asked Mrs. Bateman to submit the work to Herr Joachim for his opinion as to whether it c$^d$ be performed with fair effect by a band of the numerical dimensions of that of the Lyceum, but even if he considers it is, and incompetent performance w$^d$ of course do away with all the effect. I must have some previous guarantee that the *individual players* in this very small band will be fully competent for the task. Mrs. Bateman also says that "the entractes will be liable to interruption by the sound of the prompter's bell" a practice artistically & dramatically too reprehensible for any comment. In no performance of plays with music, and I have heard many, have I ever known of such an extraordinary proceeding. I trust you will forgive my addressing such a long letter to you on the matter: my only excuse for so doing is that I hoped to illustrate your drama as worthily as I could & I cannot but feel that to

mutilate that illustration, especially after the public has been informed that the music is forthcoming, will detract from the expected effect of the whole performance, & mar its unity, for it will involve the introduction of the ordinary irrelevant music instead of continuing the interest of the drama. Again thanking you for your part & present kindness to me believe me y$^n$. very truly
C. Villiers Stanford

## 292
## Alfred Lord Tennyson
Letter to a member of Macmillans staff
15 October ??
The Earl of Stockton

The letter reads:

Sir,
The Lady has my permission to publish "Break, break, break" with Beethoven's music.
I am, sir
Your obedient servant
A Tennyson

Tennyson's poems were often set to music, sometimes using a well-known composer, such as Beethoven, and sometimes inspiring specially composed music, as with Sullivan, Parry and Bridge. Stanford himself tells us how interested Tennyson was in the process of setting words to music:

Without being a musician, he had a great appreciation of the fitness of music to its subjects, and was an unfailing judge of musical declamation. As he expressed it himself, he disliked music which went up when it ought to go down, and went down when it ought to go up. I never knew him wrong in his suggestion on this point.[47]

# 15. Tennyson Illustrators

## Shorter Poems

### 293

**Dante Gabriel Rossetti (1828-1882)**
*Mariana*
1870
Oil on canvas 107.5 x 87.5 cms
Aberdeen Art Gallery and Museums

This painting - using Jane Morris as the model - takes Shakespeare's song from *Measure for Measure* 'Take, O take those lips away' as its epigraph, but it seems probable that Tennyson's fuller articulation of Mariana's melancholy in his poem also informs Rossetti's conception.

### 294

**James Smetham (1821-1889)**
*The Many-wintered Crow*
No date
Oil on board 15.2 x 20.3 cms
Birmingham Museums and Art Gallery

Smetham began his career as an apprentice to an artistic architect in Lincoln. He came to London in 1843, and in 1851 became drawing master at the Wesleyan Normal College, Westminster. Rossetti called his work 'the very flower of modern art'.

The title is taken from Tennyson's poem *Locksley Hall*:

Well - 'tis well that I should bluster! - Hadst thou less unworthy proved
Would to God - for I had loved thee more than ever wife was loved.

Am I mad, that I should cherish that which bears but bitter fruit?
I will pluck it from my bosom, though my heart be at the root.

Never, though my mortal summers to such length of years should come
As the many-wintered crow that leads the clanging rookery home.

### 295

**John William Inchbold (1830-1888)**
*The Moorland (Dewar-Stone, Dartmoor)*
1854
Oil on canvas 35.6 x 53.3 cms
The Tate Gallery, London

Notice the crow in the foreground, a motif that perhaps alludes to *Locksley Hall*. Other lines in the poem could describe Inchbold's painting:

Comrades, leave me here a little, while as yet 'tis early morn:
Leave me here, and when you want me, sound upon the bugle-horn.

'Tis the place, and all around it, as of old, the curlews call,
Dreary gleams the moorland flying over Locksley Hall;
Locksley Hall, that in the distance overlooks the sandy tracts,
And the hollow ocean-ridges roaring into cataracts.

### 296

**Walter Langley (1852-1922)**
*'But O for the touch of a vanished hand . . .'*
1888
Watercolour with scraping on Whatman paper
67 x 94 cms
Birmingham Museums and Art Gallery

Walter Langley was a founder of the Newlyn colony in Cornwall, and the Cornish fisherfolk remained his favourite subject. Here, he uses a typical coastal scene to illustrate Tennyson's poem 'Break, break, break'.

Break, break, break,
On thy cold gray stones, O Sea!
And I would that my tongue could utter
The thoughts that arise in me.

O well for the fisherman's boy,
That he shouts with his sister at play!
O well for the sailor lad,
That he sings in his boat on the bay!

And the stately ships go on
To their haven under the hill;
But O for the touch of a vanished hand,
And the sound of a voice that is still!

Break, break, break,
At the foot of thy crags, O Sea!
Bnt the tender grace of a day that is dead
Will never come back to me.

Only a poet of supreme rhythmical confidence could begin with three strong staccato beats like this. The monotonous and remorseless pounding of the waves is at the start and the end of the poem. There is a suggestion of baffled impossibility; the waves break against hard barriers - stones and crags - and their force, sounding and expressive though it is, conveys indifference. Their voice casts into relief the poet's own feeling of inarticulateness.

Between the first verse and last, the repeated hammering of the waves sets within a frame the activities of an ordinary world carrying on - singing, doing something, going somewhere. This normal life is rendered insignificant by the waves' great force, but at the same time it is enviable to the poet in his isolation. The themes, the words, the feelings are simple, and a part of common experience. Tennyson can raise the commonplace to art.

**297**
**Sir Edward Coley Burne-Jones (1833-1898)**
Study of the Maid for *King Cophetua and the Beggar Maid*
1883
Drawing on paper 35.2 x 24.8 cms
The Tate Gallery, London

Her arms across her breast she laid;
She was more fair than words can say:
Bare-footed came the beggar maid
Before the king Cophetua
In robe and crown the king stept down,
To meet and greet her on her way;
"It is no wonder' said the Lords,
"She is more beautiful than day.'

As shines the moon in clouded skies,
She in poor attire was seen:
One praised her ancles, one her eyes,
One her dark hair and lovesome mien.
So sweet a face, such angel grace,
In all that land had never been:
Cophetua sware a royal oath:
"This beggar maid shall be my queen."

**298**
**Sir Edward Coley Burne-Jones**
*Sisyphus*
No date
Drawing on paper 21.6 x 21.6 cms
The Tate Gallery, London

**299**
**Sir Edward Coley Burne-Jones**
Letter to Alfred Lord Tennyson
Monday [November 1881]
Tennyson Research Centre, Lincoln

Dear Mr. Tennyson
 I dont know whether the pleasure of finding you had thought of me, or disappointment at missing you was greatest yesterday. I do wish I had known beforehand - for first you should not have come on a Sunday but have had a day set apart & dedicated to you; - the first time I get into Town I will call & see if I can persuade you to come so far again, some week day; for I remember how kind you were to my poor beginnings and I should like to show you what I have done since - & possibly win a bit of praise from you.
 Before I got home and found your card I had made up my mind to write to you and ask you to come - so that finding you had been, was no little pleasure & assurance to me - believe me
Yours very truly
E Burne-Jones.

- dont trouble to answer this; but the first day I can get out this week I will call on you.

**300**
**Arthur Joseph Gaskin (1862-1928)**
*The Lady of Shalott*
1888
Pencil 29.8 x 24.1 cms
Birmingham Museums and Art Gallery

Sometimes a troop of damsels glad,
An abbot on an ambling pad,
Sometimes a curly shepherd-lad,
Or long-haired page in crimson clad,
Goes by to towered Camelot;
And sometimes through the mirror blue
The knights come riding two and two:
She hath no loyal knight and true,
The Lady of Shalott.

But in her web she still delights
To weave the mirror's magic sights,
For often through the silent nights
A funeral, with plumes and lights
And music, went to Camelot:
Or when the moon was overhead,
Came two young lovers lately wed;
'I am half sick of shadows,' said
The Lady of Shalott.

**301**
**J.A. Winter**
*The Miller's Daughter*
1859
Oil on canvas 35 x 24 cms
Wolverhampton Art Gallery

Cat. 301

302
**Matthew Webb (?1851-1924)**
*Crossing the Bar*
Gold, watercolour and gesso on paper
22.9 x 14 cms
Professor Stephen Wildman

303
**Sir John Tenniel (1820-1914)**
*Crossing the Bar*
1892
Newspaper print 46 x 36.7 cms
Lincolnshire County Council:
Tennyson Research Centre, Lincoln

A solemn cartoon from *Punch*, 15 October 1892.

304
**Alfred Lord Tennyson**
*Crossing the Bar*
1889
Holograph manuscript
Trinity College, Cambridge

Three years before his death, Tennyson wrote the poem while crossing the Solent. On his deathbed he said to Hallam: 'Mind you put "Crossing the Bar" at the end of all editions of my poems'. The poem could be considered in the context of all his work, as a defiant assertion against all the earlier religious doubts that marked his poetry. It is death that he defies.

**Crossing the Bar**

Sunset and evening star,
And one clear call for me!
And may there be no moaning of the bar,
When I put out to sea,

But such a tide as moving seems asleep,
Too full for sound and foam,
When that which drew from out the boundless deep
Turns again home.

Twilight and evening bell,
And after that the dark!
And may there be no sadness of farewell,
When I embark;

For though from out our bourne of Time and Place
The flood may bear me far,
I hope to see my Pilot face to face
When I have crost the bar.

305
**Arthur Hughes (1832-1915)**
Enoch Arden; man lying in grass
Victoria and Albert Museum

306
**Arthur Hughes**
Enoch Arden: landscape
Victoria and Albert Museum

307
**Arthur Hughes**
Enoch Arden; path in trees
Victoria and Albert Museum

308
**Arthur Hughes**
Enoch Arden; sea & promenade
Victoria and Albert Museum

309
**Arthur Hughes**
Enoch Arden; church door with grave
Victoria & Albert Museum

310
**Sir John Everett Millais**
*Go, little letter, apace . . .*
21.9 x 16.3 cms
Victoria and Albert Museum

311
**Rimer**
The Expulsion
21.3 x 13.1 cms
Victoria and Albert Museum

312
**Rimer**
The Prince in the Wood
21.3 x 13.1 cms
Victoria and Albert Museum

313
**Rimer**
The College
21.3 x 13.1 cms
Victoria and Albert Museum

314
**Sullivan**
Maud; 'When I was wont to meet her'
Victoria and Albert Museum

315
**Swain**
*Then cry peace*
Victoria and Albert Museum

## Idylls of the King

316
**Alfred Lord Tennyson**
*Enid*
Holograph manuscript
Trinity College, Cambridge

317
**Alfred Lord Tennyson**
*Idylls of the King*
Proof with manuscript
Lincolnshire County Council:
Tennyson Research Centre, Lincoln

318
**Alfred Lord Tennyson**
*Enid and Nimue*
1857 (proof copy)
Lincolnshire County Council:
Tennyson Research Centre, Lincoln

The received title became *Merlin and Vivien*.

319
**Eleanor Fortescue-Brickdale (1872-1945)**
*Guinevere*
*c.*1911
Watercolour 44.5 x 24.8 cms
Birmingham Museums and Art Gallery

Eleanor Fortescue Brickdale painted historical and genre subjects in oil, chalk and watercolour. She exhibited for the Royal Academy from 1896.

Queen Guinevere had fled the court, and sat
There in the holy house at Almesbury
Weeping, none with her save a little maid,
A novice: one low light betwixt them burned
Blurred by the creeping mist, for all abroad,
Beneath a moon unseen albeit at full,
The white mist, like a face-cloth to the face
Clung to the dead earth, and the land was still.
     (from *Guinevere* ll. 1-8)

320
**Arthur Hughes (1832-1915)**
*The Rift in the Lute*
Oil on canvas 54.7 x 92.7 cms
Carlisle Museum and Art Gallery: Tullie House

Hughes was an enthusiast of Arthurian literature. In 1860 he completed *The Knight of the Sun*, an oil on an Arthurian theme, and followed it with this painting, loosely based on *Merlin and Vivien* from Tennyson's *Idylls of the King*.

"In Love, if Love be Love, if Love be ours,
Faith and unfaith can ne'er be equal powers:
Unfaith in aught is want of faith in all.

"It is the little rift within the lute,
That by and by will make the music mute,
And ever widening slowly silence all.

"The little rift within the lover's lute
Or little pitted speck in garnered fruit,
That rotting inward slowly moulders all.

"It is not worth the keeping: let it go:
But shall it? answer, darling, answer, no.
And trust me not at all or all in all."
     (from *Merlin and Vivien*, ll. 385-396)

321
**Arthur Hughes**
Study for *The Rift in the Lute*
No date
Pencil and brown ink on paper 3.6 x 8.5 cms
Fitzwilliam Museum

322
**Sir Edward Coley Burne-Jones**
*Launcelot at the Chapel of the Holy Grail*
1883
Oil on canvas 138.5 x 169.8 cms
Southampton Art Gallery

Lancelot is unable to enter the Chapel of the Holy Grail, but later his son Galahad has the pure spirit to encounter it.

          up I climb'd a thousand steps
With pain: as in a dream I seem'd to climb
For ever: at the last I reach'd a door,
A light was in the crannies, and I heard,
'Glory and joy and honour to our Lord
And to the Holy Vessel of the Grail.'
Then in my madness I essay'd the door;
It gave; and thro' a stormy glare, a heat
As from a seventimes-heated furnace, I,
Blasted and burnt, and blinded as I was,
With such a fierceness that I swoon'd away -
O, yet methought I saw the Holy Grail,
All pall'd in crimson samite, and around
Great angels, awful shapes, and wings and eyes.
And but for all my madness and my sin,
And then my swooning, I had sworn I saw
That which I saw; but what I saw was veil'd
And cover'd; and this Quest was not for me."

323
**Sir Edward Coley Burne-Jones**
Sketchbook
*c.*1874
Pencil on off white paper
Fitzwilliam Museum

The book contains a brilliantly detailed pencil study for his large oil, 'Merlin and Vivien' (indeed, it is entirely devoted to drapery studies for the figure of Vivien). His method of using wet draperies on the model is clearly shown.

Cat. 323

324

**Alfred Lord Tennyson**
*Elaine*
Illustrated by Gustave Doré
London: Edward Moxon and C°, 1867
Lincolnshire County Council:
Tennyson Research Centre, Lincoln

325

**Alfred Lord Tennyson**
*The Story of Elaine*
Illustrated by Gustave Doré
London: E. Moxon and C°, 1871
Lincolnshire County Council:
Tennyson Research Centre, Lincoln

The two volumes differ in their style of engraving.

326

**James Archer (1823-1904)**
*The Dying King Arthur*
Oil on canvas 36.5 x 54 cms
Pre-Raphaelite Inc. (by courtesy of Julian Hartnoll)

327

**William Ernest Reynolds-Stephens (1862-1943)**
*Sir Lancelot and the Nestling*
1899
Bronze, ivory, mother-of-pearl and enamel H 86cm
Pre-Raphaelite Inc. (by courtesy of Julian Hartnoll)

328

**William Ernest Reynolds-Stephens**
*Guinevere and the Nestling*
1900
Bronze, ivory, mother-of-pearl and enamel H 86cm
Pre-Raphaelite Inc. (by courtesy of Julian Hartnoll)

Reynolds-Stephens was born in Detroit of British parents, and came to England as a child. On his death in 1943 *The Times* obituary described him as 'a belated Pre-Raphaelite. He liked Romantic subjects such as *Guinevere's Redemption, Lancelot and the Nestling* and *The Sleeping Beauty*, and he was true to the tradition of the school in practising a great variety of arts and crafts.' *The Athenaeum* described the *Lancelot* as his 'best work. . .combining stateliness and grace', and in both sculptures his skill in the working of mixed materials is very evident.

Tennyson recounts the story of the nestling in *The Last Tournament*, part of his *Idylls of the King*.

For Arthur and Sir Lancelot riding once
Far down beneath a winding wall of rock
Heard a child wail. A stump of oak half-dead,
From roots like some black coil of carven snakes,

Clutched at the crag, and started through mid air
Bearing an eagle's nest: and through the tree
Rushed ever a rainy wind, and through the wind
Pierced ever a child's cry: and crag and tree
Scaling, Sir Lancelot from the perilous nest,
This ruby necklace thrice around her neck,
And all unscarred from beak or talon, brought
A maiden babe; which Arthur pitying took,
Then gave it to his Queen to rear: the Queen
But coldly acquiescing, in her white arms
Received, and after loved it tenderly,
And named it Nestling; so forgot herself
A moment, and her cares
　　(*The Last Tournament*, ll. 10-26)

329

**George Frampton (1860-1928)**
*Enid the Fair*
1907
Bronze H 51cm
Matthieson Fine Art Ltd., London

Again, the subject is from one of Tennyson's *The Idylls of King*. George Frampton, Royal Academician and founder-member of the Royal Society of British Sculptors, had a long-lasting interest in the Arthurian legend, and in the latter part of his career produced a number of idealised, decorative bronze heads of its heroines.

But Enid, whom her ladies loved to call
Enid the fair, a grateful people named
Enid the Good; and in their halls arose
The cry of children, Enids and Geraints
Of times to be; nor did he doubt her more,
But rested in her fealty, till he crowned
A happy life with a fair death, and fell
Against the heathen of the Northern Sea
In battle, fighting for the blameless King.
　　(*Geraint and Enid* ll. 961-969)

330

**The Ascot Jubilee Cup**
Henry Hugh Armstead
1887
Silver
Pre-Raphaelite Inc. (by courtesy of Julian Hartnoll)

The cup was described in the *Illustrated London News* of 11 June, 1887 in the following terms:

The Royal Jubilee Cup, won at Ascot races on Tuesday by the colt Minting, of which Mr Vyner is the owner, is a beautiful vase, manufactured by Messrs. Hancocks & Co., of Bruton Street, New Bond Street, and is valued at £1,000. It was modelled by Mr. H.H. Armstead, R.A., whose design is illustrative of scenes and characters in Lord Tennyson's noblest "Idylls of the King", the story of Guinevere and the "Morte d'Arthur". The front medallion represents the conflict between King Arthur and Modred:

"King am I, whatsoever be their cry:

And one last act of kinghood shalt thou see
Yet ere I pass." And uttering this the King
Made at the man: then Modred smote his liege
Hard on that helm which many a heathen sword
Had beaten thin: while Arthur at one blow,
Striking the last blow with Excalibur,
Slew him, and all but slain himself, he fell.

The other medallion represents King Arthur being conveyed on the barge:

Then murmured Arthur "Place me in the barge";
So to the barge they came. There those three Queens
Put forth their hands, and took the King, and wept.
But she, that rose the tallest of them all
And fairest; laid his head upon her lap,
And loosed the shatter'd casque, and chaff'd his hands,
And called him by his name, complaining loud.

The figures on the handle are those of Queen Guinevere and the enchanter Merlin. The ornamentation is Byzantine Gothic of the twelfth Century.

Cat. 330

# 16. Edward Lear

Edward Lear (1812-1888), the artist and nonsense poet, was a later friend of Tennyson, whose affectionate poem 'To E.L. on his Travels in Greece' (published 1853) is addressed to him. But Lear was more devoted to Emily Tennyson than to the poet himself, and he sometimes thought Tennyson was somewhat careless of his wife's feelings. Even so, Lear's letters, with their determined humour and nostalgic reminiscence, reveal how he found life at Farringford, the Tennysons' home on the Isle of Wight, a refreshing respite from his wandering, bachelor existence.

## To E.L. on his Travels in Greece

Illyrian woodlands, echoing falls
    Of water, sheets of summer glass,
    The long divine Peneïan pass,
The vast Akrokeraunian walls,

Tomohrit, Athos, all things fair,
    With such a pencil, such a pen,
    You shadow forth to distant men,
I read, and felt that I was there:

And trust me while I turned the page,
    And tracked you still on classic ground,
    I grew in gladness till I found
My spirits in the golden age.

For me the torrent ever poured
    And glistened - here and there alone
    The broad-limbed Gods at random thrown
By fountain-urns; - and Naiads oared

A glimmering shoulder under gloom
    Of cavern pillars; on the swell
    The silver lily heaved and fell;
And many a slope was rich in bloom

From him that on the mountain lea
    By dancing rivulets fed his flocks
    To him who sat upon the rocks,
And fluted to the morning sea.

## 331
**Edward Lear**
*'Faringford'*
Dated 15 October 1864
Watercolour, bodycolour, pencil, pen
36 x 48.5 cms
Lincolnshire County Council:
Tennyson Research Centre, Lincoln

Emily Tennyson enters in her journal on 1 October 1864:

Mr. Lear arrives. A most beautiful day & he is charmed & makes a sketch on the South side. . . . It is very pleasant to see Mr. Lear so well & cheerful. He interests A. & me very much by his talk of Crete & other countries & other things.

Lear characteristically writes notes on his drawings and adds a comic touch: a large beetle walks over the lawn.

## 332
**Edward Lear**
Letter to Lady Tennyson
28-29 October 1855
Lincolnshire County Council:
Tennyson Research Centre, Lincoln

My dear Mrs Tennyson,

At times, ever since last Sunday, - I have had responsible twinges for never having written to you: but I have never had real leisure, or, if I had any, I was all jarry & out of time & you would not have thanked me for scribbling ever so little. Not that what I have thought of Faringford at all times and seasons ever since I left, & this morning I see everything - even to the plate of mushrooms: then Hallam & Lionel come in, - & when they are gone, you, Alfred & Frank begin to talk like Gods together careless of mankind: - & so on, all through the day. According to the morbid nature of the animal, I even complain sometimes that such rare flashes of light as such visits are to me, make the path darker after they are over: - a bright blue & green landscape with purple hills, & winding rivers, & unexplored forests, and airy downs, & trees & birds, & all sorts of calm repose, - exchange for a dull dark plain horizonless, pathless, & covered with cloud above while well beneath are brambles & weariness.

I really do believe that I enjoy hardly any one thing on earth while it is present: - always looking back, or frettingly peering into the dim beyond. - With all this, I must say to you & Alfred, that the 3 or 4 of the 16 - 20th October/55, - were the best I have passed for many a long day. - If I live to grow old, & can hope to exist in England, I should like to be somewhere near you in one's later days. I wish sometimes you could settle near Park House. Then I might have a room in Boxley, & moon cripply cripply about those hills, & sometimes see by turns Hallam & Lionel's children, & Frank's grandchildren, & so slide pleasantly out of life. Alfred, by that time would have written endlessly, & there would be 6 or 8 thick green volumes of poems. I possibly, - should be in the workhouse, but I know you would all come & see me.

Now: - I won't write any more nonsense, but be all statistic & beautiful common sense. The sail from Yarmouth to Lymington on the 20th was most quiet & pleasant, & as successful a boating trip as F's & my last, previous one, from Lepanto to Patras. At Brockenhurst FL went out to Bouchiers, - I homeward, - or, more truly to speak, to my empty lodgings where 3 chairs a coalscuttle & a table are the prevailing furniture.

Since then, I have been a good deal here, - at the home of my old friend (6 miles from town,) to parents of a little godchild. They are very kind to me always, & are frantic Tennysonians in many ways, are, to be continually forcing me to sing for hours at a time. Other Evenings I go to some friends, Beaden the Police Magistrate, whose house in Stratford Place is always open to me. There one learns that some are born to know sorrows above common comprehension - for their earliest friends are the Bankers Strahan & c - & in their present wretchedness, poor Mrs S.- (left with 9 children, & by yesterdays verdict, seeing her husband transported for 14 years,) finds a home. In the day time I work at the picture of Philoe which progresses but slowly. My sister Ann comes frequently & sits for 4 or 5 hours. -

I shall hardly get away before the middle of November: - & FL who writes yesterday, though he says nothing of any house, alludes to the Cholera having broken out at Corfu. Will this, I think, make any difference as to Ellen's going? - Anyhow I do not change my plans. - I have no fear of contagion, but I grieve & believe that the knowledge of that epidemic being in the Island, will throw one more shade on to the solitary pathways at Park House when Frank is gone.

I *must* go down there once more before I go, - if it is only to tell Ellen, (should it be finally decided that she stays,) that I go with, & shall [?] her brother. But I shall only walk over from Maidstone, & not stay there. The account of Eddy seems to me better. Frank himself is certainly greatly improved in health: - and if Ellen could but go with him all would seem brighter.

As for me, I have to look forward to a new beginning of life: but it is much much pleasanter than I had believed it possible by help from others, as to commissions for drawings.

O dear! I cant write any more now for noise. But I will write again ere long.

Kind love to Alfred, & believe me
Dear Mrs Tennyson
Yours very sincerely
Edward Lear

### 333
**Edward Lear**
Letter to Lady Tennyson
5 January 1876
Lincolnshire County Council:
Tennyson Research Centre, Lincoln

My dear Mrs Tennyson,

I find an old Envelope, intended to be filled up to you thousands of years ago: (but I cant write by Lamplight in these latter days & the whole daylight is crowded with work, - so though constantly intentioning to write letters never get written;) - & as Frank has just told me that Lionel is really engaged to Miss Locker, I shall use the ancient Letter even to send my Congratulations to you & AT not to speak of the principal party concerned. But I must tell you that

I
I
I
ME
MYSELF
Edward Lear

was the indivigual who told Frank of the fact that - & this forestalled Lionels communication. How it came about I shall not say, except that a Lady a friend of mine, wrote to me that a Lady a friend of hers had told her; whereby I wrote to F. L - & he wrote to Lionel, & Lionel to him, & I to you --- on the principle of the House that Jack built.

I knew the young Lady's mother in Palermo years ago, & am glad to know that the young couple are likely to be so happy. But I hope he will *do* something by way of profession, & not dawdle with idleness. If I had sons, I would make them Fishmungers or Lettercarriers, - or Coalheavers rather than nothing.

My love to Everybody.
Your affectionately,
Edward Lear.

### 334
**Edward Lear**
Letter to Hallam Tennyson
8 September 1885
Lincolnshire County Council:
Tennyson Research Centre, Lincoln

My dear Hallam

*The* Photograph arrived quite safely yesterday Evening, & I am delighted with it. I am so much obliged to you. I always felt sure she had beautiful eyes, in spite of the 1st Photograph which probably was so arranged by the wife or other feminine party belonging to the Photographer who had got ugly eyes, & was jealous of all pretty ones. As soon as I get back to Sanremo I shall have the likeness framed; the face is so charming that even if it belonged to Mrs Peregrine Pobbsquobb or anyone else & not Hallam Tennyson's wife it would be a lovely portrait to look at. The arrangement of the hair is perfect; - how strange that 9 out of 10 women cannot see that such a simple matter improves their beauty & on the contrary prefer nourishing Goat Curls & other hideousnesses! Thank you my dear boy, and likewise give my thanks to your Audrey - for you have both given me a real pleasure.

I leave here tomorrow & return to my native 'ome at Sanremo - going by Milan & Savona - a railway journey I dread & detest - for I am but very feeble. The Mundellas were coming to see me tomorrow but I wrote to put them off & we meet at Milan: it is so wet here now that there is not fun for the time being.

I send to Sanremo 120 of my 200 Tennyson illustrations, these 120 now pretty well completed. More about the whole work at a fewcher thyme.

I have just had a very nice letter from your Uncle Edmund, & have made a confidence to him (& to the D of Argyll - with whom I am in correspondence about certain Nile stratifications) which I shall repeat to you in

Cat. 346

Cat. 346

worse, on the next leaf.

I often think of you all at Aldworth & should like to be there. Give my love to your mother & father & to the Lionels & to your Audrey.

You are fortunate indeed to be so happy in marriage, yet I fancy the happiness is well meritted if only for your Father & Mother's sake - not to speak of your own, which you are by no means a bad cove.

Good bye my dear Hallam

Yours affectionately, Edward Lear.

1

When leaving this beautiful blessèd Brianza
   My trunks were all corded & locked except one;
But that was unfilled, through a dismal mancanza,
   Nor could I determine on what should be done.

2

For, out of *three* volumes, (all equally bulky,)
   Which - travelling, - I constantly carry about,
There was room but for *two*. So, though angry & sulky,
   I had to decide as to which to leave out.

3

A Bible! a Shakespeare! a Tennyson! - stuffing
   And cramming and squeezing were wholly in vain.
- A Tennyson! - Shakespeare! and Bible! - all puffing
   Was useless, and *one* of the *three must* remain.

4

And this was the end, (as is truth & no libel;-)
   Aweary with thinking I settled my doubt
As I packed & sent off both the Shakespeare & Bible
   And finally left the "Lord Tennyson" *out*!

Villa Figini. Barzano
8 Sept 1885

## Illustrations

Lear had an almost obsessive desire to produce a complete edition of Tennyson's works, which he had revered since the appearance of the 1842 *Poems*. Unlike many of the artists of his generation, he saw that Tennyson's poetry could be illustrated by landscapes, rather than character studies. On 5 October 1852 he wrote to Emily Tennyson:

My desire has been to show that Alfred Tennyson's poetry (with regard to scenes - ) is as real and exquisite as it is relatively to higher and deeper matters - that his descriptions of certain spots are as positively true as if drawn from the places themselves, and that his words have the power of calling up images as distinct and correct as if they were written from those images, instead of giving rise to them.

Lear described his life as 'a series of pictures seen through "Memory's Arch"'; by matching Tennyson's poetic images with landscapes he knew from his own extensive travels abroad, he could relive his own past. His aim was to pay tribute to the poetry, but it was also, more importantly, to achieve a spiritual journey of his own.

335
**Edward Lear**
Enoch Arden's island
No date
Watercolour, pen and pencil 24.3 x 44 cms
Lincolnshire County Council:
Tennyson Research Centre, Lincoln

336
**Edward Lear**
Plain of Thebes, Egypt
&
Untitled imaginary landscape
No date
Pen and grey wash 14.6 x 9.5 cms
Ruth Pitman Collection

337
**Edward Lear**
The Monastery of Ma Saba, Jordan
No date
Watercolour 10.2 x 19.7 cms
Whitworth Art Gallery, Manchester

338
**Edward Lear**
Telecherry. Malabar
&
Mar Sabbas. Palastine
No date
Pen and grey wash 14.6 x 9.5 cms
Bristol University

339
**Edward Lear**
Kasr es Saad. Nile. Egypt
&
Lake of Luro. Epirus. Albania
No date
Pen and grey wash 14.6 x 9.5 cms
Bristol University

340
**Edward Lear**
Pass of Mount Tchilla. Akrokeraunian Mountains.
Albania
&
Akrokeraunian mountains. Draghiades (Khimara).
Albania
No date
Pen and grey wash 14.6 x 9.5 cms
Bristol University

341
**Edward Lear**
Cape St. Angelo Amalfi, Italy
&
Coast of Gozo, Malta
No date
Pen and grey wash 14.6 x 9.5 cms
Ruth Pitman Collection

342
**Edward Lear**
Philae, Egypt
&
Philae, Egypt
No date
Pen and grey wash 14.6 x 9.5 cms
Ruth Pitman Collection

343
**Edward Lear**
Stᵃ. Maria si Polsi Calabria. Italy
&
Blithfield Staffordshire, England
No date
Pen and grey wash 14.6 x 9.5 cms
Ruth Pitman Collection

344
**Edward Lear**
Akrokeraunian Mountains, (Chimara) Albania
&
Akrokeraunian Mountains, (Chimera) Albania
No date
Pen and grey wash 14.6 x 9.5 cms
Ruth Pitman Collection

345
**Edward Lear**
Petra Palestine
&
Cape St. Angelo Corfu. Greece
No date
Pen and grey wash 14.6 x 9.5 cms
Ruth Pitman Collection

346
**Edward Lear and Frederick Underhill**
Group of lithographs
Campbell Fine Art

*The Dying Swan*
16.9 x 26.2 cms

*The Dying Swan*
16.9 x 26.2 cms

*Oenone / Bavella, Corsica*
17 x 26.2 cms

*Locksley Hall / Kinchinjunga, Darjeeling*
16.9 x 26.4 cms

*The Palace of Art Pentedaleto*
16.6 x 26.1 cms

Lear was constantly experimenting with different ways of reproducing his work. This extremely rare group of lithographs dates from 1885, when Lear invited the talented lithographer, Frederick Underhill, to San Remo to assist him in reproducing some trial lithographs based upon his monochrome sketches.

347
**Edward Lear**
Letter to Lady Tennyson (incomplete)
No date
Lincolnshire County Council:
Tennyson Research Centre, Lincoln

. . . as many as, 12 - advanced as far as the 5th stage of their queer existence - all in Umber & dark - but having a bodily & poetical entity. 2. in Oenone. 2 in Lotos Eaters. 2 in V. of fair women. 1. in 2 voices, and 5 in palace of art.-

Besides them I shall hope to bring 10 or 13 in their 3d or advanced caterpillar stage - & thus you will perceive substantially what is intended for just one half of the whole set. -

One subject (from 2 voices) I got yesterday by walking 10 miles - "the village Yew" - & that never went through the early stages of its foolish life not at all - but burst forth in its fifth phase all at once after the fashion of grasshoppers & the insects who wholly disapprove of & repudiate the chrysalis & caterpillar department of infancy.

I shall be very grieved if I cannot carry out the scheme - i.e. if I really commit myself to it out & out, but it will require no little patience & application & trouble, for I must go to Cornwall & other places on purpose. The *most difficult* [?] to be overcome is my own instability of pupose. - If I succeed in making *good* illustrations to his poems, - (& I shall never wish to see them or suffer them to be engraved unless they quite fulfil my idea of - as it were "translations" of the quotations, - ) I shall be exceedingly delighted.

I have resolved on *not* doing anything like "the Moated Grange" - or "the 7 elms the poplars 6 -" - from spots near or similar to those said to be the ones T. has described. . .

I sit sometimes & think of the horrible elevation of bumptiousness to which I must have arrived before I could fancy I could do this properly! . . .

348
**Alfred Lord Tennyson**
*Tiresias*
London: E. Moxon, 1885
George Mandl Collection

Inscribed by the author to Edward Lear.

# 17. Julia Margaret Cameron (1815-1879)

Her husband, Charles Hay Cameron (1795-1880), a scholar and a lawyer who worked in her native Calcutta and in Ceylon, came to live on the Isle of Wight in 1860. It was then that Julia Margaret Cameron took up photography. Her reputation rests on the quality of her portrait work. George Bernard Shaw, as art critic for *The Star*, wrote in 1889:

While the portraits of Herschel, Tennyson and Carlyle beat hollow anything I have ever seen, right on the same wall, and virtually in the same frame, there are photographs of children with no clothes on, or else the underclothes by way of propriety, with palpably paper wings, most inartistically grouped and artlessly labelled as angels, saints or fairies. No-one would imagine that the artist who produced the marvellous Carlyle would have produced such childish trivialities.[48]

## Portraiture

349
**Frederick Tennyson (1807-1898)**
Portrait by Julia Margaret Cameron
*c.*1865
Photograph 25.6 x 20.8 cms
Lincolnshire County Council:
Tennyson Research Centre, Lincoln

Frederick Tennyson, the eldest son of George Clayton Tennyson, closely resembled his father in temperament, and often quarrelled violently with him. In 1835 he travelled to Italy, and made it his home for the next twenty-three years. In Florence he met Robert Browning, and the two became close friends. In later life he found Tennyson's fame hard to accept, and in particular found Emily Tennyson snobbish and over-ambitious for his brother.

350
**Horatio Tennyson (1819-1899)**
Portrait by Julia Margaret Cameron
1867
Photograph 34.4 x 26.8 cms
Lincolnshire County Council:
Tennyson Research Centre, Lincoln

Horatio Tennyson never took on a profession; his attempt to earn a living by farming in Tasmania soon was abandoned. Edward Fitzgerald described him as 'rather unused to the planet'. 'One day he was to go to Cheltenham, another to Plymouth; then he waited for an umbrella he thought he had left somewhere. So where he is now I have no notion.'

Cat. 349

Cat. 350

**351**

**James Spedding (1808-1881)**
Portrait by Julia Margaret Cameron
1864
Photograph 25.4 x 20.2 cms
Spedding Collection

**352**

**Aubrey de Vere (1814-1902)**
Portrait by Julia Margaret Cameron
No date
Photograph 10 x 6.3 cms
Lincolnshire County Council:
Tennyson Research Centre, Lincoln

**353**

**Aubrey de Vere**
Portrait by Julia Margaret Cameron
No date
Photograph 10 x 6.3 cms
Lincolnshire County Council:
Tennyson Research Centre, Lincoln

**354**

**Aubrey de Vere**
Letter to Alfred Lord Tennyson
26 October 1889
Lincolnshire County Council:
Tennyson Research Centre, Lincoln

My dear Alfred

I send you the enclosed poem because I think that you have never published it, & possibly have not a copy of it. The history of it will amuse you. R N Milnes came here in 1832, & introduced us to your poetry. Among other poems of yours which he read aloud to us was this sonnet then in M S. which however he refused to give us a copy of. My sister then wrote out as you will see the whole of it from memory to his great amazement. He could not prevent her from keeping what she had thus won, & was contented with her promise that no copy of it be ever taken. You will remember my bringing you to her house near the falls of the Shannon at Castle Connell, that night when the moon swelled out to the size of four moons, as if she had drawn nearer than usual to see what an English Poet looked like - having seen no other since Spenser, whose Faery Queene was composed among the moonlight forests of old Desmond.

I wish you would publish this Sonnet in your new volume, first because it is a singularly fine one (I remember well my father's admiration of it, and especially of its *abrupt* beginning with the word "therefore") & secondly because it is a most salutary reproof much more needed now than when it was written. At that time the evil consisted chiefly in neglect: since the changes made within the last few years an absolutely false Principle has utterly overthrown the Ideal of old times viz that expressed by the Motto of Oxford, "Dominus Illuminatio Mea": & I believe that in most of

our University Colleges, including Trinity Coll. Dublin, the Teachers to whom the young men look up with the unsuspecting reverence of youth for intellect & learning, may be now or may become, nearly all of them, *avowed* Agnostics or Aetheists. I find it more difficult to forgive Gladstone for his connivence with this change (his own sympathies having always been with Religious Education) than for all he has done to keep on that Revolution which tries its "Prentice Hand" on Ireland, but will not stop there.

Soon after I saw you I passed a night as usual at Card. Newman - now into his 90th year & week in body but strong in mind. His face seemed to me radient with charity & peace; & his smile was a mystery of sweetness such as I have never seen on any other face. He spoke strongly against the progress of Democracy - much also about both Poetry & Religion. Respecting "Eternal Punishment" he made a memorable distinction. He said, the Church regards the *Loss* of God the *Poena Damni*, as Eternal: but a Catholic is free to regard the other Penalty, viz "*Poena Sensus*" as temporary. It is I think this last, viz the *Poena Sensus* is that - often spoken so strongly by you. Adieu & God bless you.

With much love to all,
affectionately yours
Aubrey de Vere

**355**

**Benjamin Jowett (1817-93)**
Portrait by Julia Margaret Cameron
No date
Photograph 24.3 x 19.8 cms
Lincolnshire County Council:
Tennyson Research Centre, Lincoln

Jowett was the Master of Balliol who became one of Tennyson's most sympathetic friends. For some of his shrewd comments see the notes to *Locksley Hall* and 'O that 'twere possible'.

**356**

**Thomas Carlyle (1795-1881)**
Portrait by Julia Margaret Cameron
*c.*1867
Photograph 30.1 x 25 cms
Lincolnshire County Council:
Tennyson Research Centre, Lincoln

Tennyson was aware of Carlyle, both through his work and his conversation. Where Carlyle becomes more and more the failed prophet as years go by, Tennyson rises in public esteem and popularity. In the end Tennyson is to be rejected by the sage: 'His *Princess*, a gorgeous piece of writing but to me new melancholy proof of the futility of what they call "art". Alas! Alfred too, I fear will prove one of the *sacrificed*, and in very deed it is a pity'. *Maud*, when it appeared in 1855, was declared a 'cobweb'. He would not listen to Tennyson's reading of that poem, but took a walk. When Tennyson's *Idylls* appeared Carlyle considered them merely 'spinning rhymes'.

'When I have had such men before my camera,' writes Julia Margaret Cameron, my whole soul has endeavoured to do its duty towards them in recording faithfully the greatness of the inner as well as the features of the outer man.'[49]

**357**
**George Frederic Watts (1817-1904)**
Portrait by Julia Margaret Cameron
*c.*1865
Photograph 25.1 x 20.2 cms
Lincolnshire County Council:
Tennyson Research Centre, Lincoln

**358**
**George Frederic Watts**
Portrait by Julia Margaret Cameron
*c.*1865
Photograph H 21.2 cms
Lincolnshire County Council:
Tennyson Research Centre, Lincoln

**359**
**George Frederic Watts**
Portrait by Julia Margaret Cameron
No date
Photograph 25.3 x 20 cms
Lincolnshire County Council:
Tennyson Research Centre, Lincoln

**360**
**Robert Browning (1812-89)**
Portrait by Julia Margaret Cameron
*c.*1868
Photograph 20.9 x 19.6 cms
Lincolnshire County Council:
Tennyson Research Centre, Lincoln

**361**
**Robert Browning**
Letter to Alfred Lord Tennyson
13 December 1885
Lincolnshire County Council:
Tennyson Research Centre, Lincoln

My dear Tennyson,
 Some five days ago, when my sister, opening an evening paper, startled me with "Why - he has dedicated his book to "his good friend R. B."! I said "Sir, my good friend - I'll change that name with you": I loved him always, and have venerated his genius fifty years long. Presently the Post brought the book itself, and I could read the gracious continuation of those two precious and all sufficient words. They seem, however, to claim a sort

of judgement on the poems they precede: will it be enough to say that what I "best appreciate" in these is the triumphant evidence they afford that the poet's excellence is supreme as ever; while my "allowance for the worst" goes so far as to admit that yet another year may be no unreasonable time to wait before such another proof of it comes to gladden heart and glorify soul. "Tiresias" seems a break-off bit of the old rock-crystal, but the "Ancient Sage" is "one entire and perfect chrysolite", engraved so that, besides a jewel, it is grown a talisman. And what praise and thanks shall requite you for "To-morrow", and the delicious Spinster with her Robby and Stevie? (Two evenings ago, Millais, at the mention of this letter, threw back his head and up his eyes with the rapturious expression of a connoisseur at the uncorking of a bottle of true Thirty-four.)
 My dear Tennyson, God bless you and continue to all who know you the blessing of your life and work. Tell Lady Tennyson something of what I feel about you both. When, last August, I was preparing to go abroad, I made up my mind to do a long deferred duty, and spent three mornings in destroying letters. I came upon and could not harm one syllable of one the kindest in the world, which put at the disposal of my wife, had she been able to profit by the offer, your house at Twickenham, your servants, all that was yours and her own to give. Life is well worth living were it only for such an experience and all that it implies. Give my love to Hallam too, whom, not long after, I was to see baptized . . .
Ever affectionately yours
Robert Browning

**362**
**Sir Henry Taylor (1800-86)**
Portrait by Julia Margaret Cameron
*c.*1865
Photograph 25.6 x 20.1 cms
Lincolnshire County Council:
Tennyson Research Centre, Lincoln

Before she met Tennyson, for Julia Margaret Cameron the first of living poets was Henry Taylor, and hence he was a frequent subject of her photographic studies: sometimes he was himself, but at others he was theatrically placed as 'Prospero' or 'King David'. He was evidently a willing sitter:

Our chief friend, Sir Henry Taylor, lent himself greatly to my early efforts. Regardless of the possible dread that sitting to my fancy might be making a fool of himself, he, with greatness which belongs to unselfish affection, consented to be in turn Friar Laurence with Juliet, Prospero with Miranda, Ahasuerus with Queen Esther, to hold my poker as his sceptre, and do whatever I desired of him.[50]

363

**Sir Henry Taylor**
Portrait by Julia Margaret Cameron
No date
Photograph
Lincolnshire County Council:
Tennyson Research Centre, Lincoln

364

**Sir Henry Taylor**
Portrait by Julia Margaret Cameron
*c.*1865
Photograph 35.9 x 27.4 cms
Lincolnshire County Council:
Tennyson Research Centre, Lincoln

365

**Sir Henry Taylor as Prospero**
Portrait by Julia Margaret Cameron
*c.*1867
Photograph 28 x 22 cms
Lincolnshire County Council:
Tennyson Research Centre, Lincoln

366

**Sir Henry Taylor as King David**
Portrait by Julia Margaret Cameron
*c.*1867
Photograph 26.8 x 21.1 cms
Lincolnshire County Council:
Tennyson Research Centre, Lincoln

367

**Alfred Lord Tennyson**
Letter to Sir Henry Taylor
23 March 1885
Lincolnshire County Council:
Tennyson Research Centre, Lincoln

Tennyson upbraids Taylor for making fun of Julia
Margaret Cameron in his autobiography.

My dear Sir Henry
I have seen the notice of your work in the Times & can
but express my regret that by quoting that letter from my
dear old friend Mrs Cameron, you have cared to show to
the world one, who worshipt you, as totally deficient in
humour. It is very possible that I went on in the
rollicking way after dinner, saying I was afraid of you &
that every crime was atributable to autograph-hunters. I
can quite fancy myself saying it, but I could never have
imagined that such a man as yourself would have so far
chimed in with the bad taste of the age, as to have
published her letter - dear old Julia Cameron -
Yours (as I said before) regretfully
Tennyson

They lately sold at Public Auction the love-letters of
John Keats for more than £500 - the sweat & agony of

his heart was worth so much gold. If I could fancy that
the clear & noble spirit of you, my old friend, were
touched even by the penumbra of such business, I could
only bow my head in shame, & wish that I had never
written a line.

368

**William Michael Rossetti**
Portrait by Julia Margaret Cameron
No date
Photograph 25.2 x 20.3 cms
Lincolnshire County Council:
Tennyson Research Centre, Lincoln

369

**William Michael Rossetti**
Portrait by Julia Margaret Cameron
No date
Photograph 25.2 x 20.1 cms
Lincolnshire County Council:
Tennyson Research Centre, Lincoln

After the sitting Julia Margaret Cameron wrote
impulsively to Rossetti on 23 January 1866:

I have heard *from* you and only once *of* you since the
afternoon when you devotedly did your best *for* me and
I in turn did my best with you, for I verily believe I have
never had more remarkable success with any photograph,
but I should like to know if you yourself are of this
opinion for I have never heard even whether you approve
of the picture![51]

W.M. Rossetti was the brother of Dante Gabriel
and Christina Rossetti. His good looks were shared
by his uncle, Dr. John Polidori, the author of *The
Vampyre* (1819) and once Byron's doctor.

370

**W.H. Brookfield (1809-74)**
Portrait by Julia Margaret Cameron
*c.*1865
Photograph H 21.9 cms
Lincolnshire County Council:
Tennyson Research Centre, Lincoln

371

**Mary Hillier**
Portrait by Julia Margaret Cameron
*c.*1866
Photograph 8.8 x 5.7 cms
Lincolnshire County Council:
Tennyson Research Centre, Lincoln

Mary Hiller was a local girl, Mrs. Cameron's
parlourmaid, and her most regular model. She was
known locally as 'Island Mary' and as 'Mary
Madonna', two roles she often played in the
photographs. Julia Margaret Cameron wrote to
Pinkie Ritchie on 14 May 1872:

Those only who don't know you in all your expressions think them idealized just as so many think I idealise and glorify my beautiful Madonna [Mary Hillier] but I know all her expressions - and know all the beauty and I nearly fixed for ever what I saw of you in the glass house but then movement comes because you are not *yet* so practised a sitter as my Angel of the Tomb [Mary Hillier].[52]

**372**
**Unknown artist**
Tennyson meeting Garibaldi
1864
Newspaper print 29 x 24 cms
Lincolnshire County Council:
Tennyson Research Centre, Lincoln

Garibaldi was one of the few subjects whom Julia Margaret Cameron failed to persuade to sit for her. Emily Tennyson writes in her Journal:

We introduced Garibaldi to Sir Henry Taylor and to some of our other friends. . . . Mrs. Cameron wanted to photograph Garibaldi, and dropped down on her knees before him, and held up her black hands, covered with chemicals. He evidently thought that she was a beggar and turned away, until we explained who she was.

## Idylls

In 1875 Julia Margaret Cameron published her last major project, a series of photographs depicting scenes from Tennyson's *Idylls of the King*. The studies range between the ludicrous and the inspired, but are representative of the widespread Victorian practice of playing scenes from Tennyson's works, and, according to Julia Margaret Cameron, it was Tennyson's own idea that she illustrate the *Idylls of the King*. On 4 December 1874 she wrote to Sir Edward Ryan:

Alfred Tennyson *asked* me to illustrate his Idylls *for his people's edition* and when I had achieved my beautiful large pictures at such a cost of labor, strength and money, for I have taken 245 photographs to get these twelve successes, it seemed such a pity that they should only appear in the very tiny reduced form in Alfred's volume (where I gave them only as a matter of friendship), that he himself said to me "Why don't you bring them out in their actual size in a big volume at your own risk" and I resolved at once to do so'.[53]

Usually Tennyson hated his work to be illustrated, but the desire to see photographic presentations of Arthurian scenes next to the *Idylls* is perhaps not unexpected from a man who had, according to James Spedding in 1835, an 'almost personal dislike of the present, whatever it may be.'

**373**
**Julia Margaret Cameron**
*Illustrations for Alfred Tennyson's Idylls of the King and other Poems*
London: Henry S. King & Co. 1875
Lincolnshire County Council:
Tennyson Research Centre, Lincoln

This folio volume contains twelve signed and titled illustrations to Tennyson's *Idylls of the King*. The 'Dirty Monk' portrait serves as frontispiece. The poems are interleaved with excerpts from the poems lithographed from Julia Margaret Cameron's handwriting. It was followed a few months later by a second and even rarer volume. The illustrations, which measure on average 13 3/4 x 12 1/2 ", are as follows:

1. Frontispiece of Tennyson, 'The Dirty Monk'
2. "Gareth and Lynette"
3. "Enid" *(Geraint and Enid)*
4. "And Enid Sang" *(Geraint and Enid)*
5. "Vivien and Merlin" *(Merlin and Vivien)*
6. "Vivien and Merlin"
7. "Elaine the lily maid of Astolat" *(Lancelot and Elaine)*
8. "Elaine"
9. "Sir Galahad and the pale nun" *(The Holy Grail)*
10. "The parting of Lancelot and Guinevere"
11. "The little novice and the Queen at the Holy House at Almesbury" *(Guinevere)*
12. "King Arthur"
13. "The Passing of Arthur"

**374**
**Julia Margaret Cameron**
*Illustrations by Julia Margaret Cameron for Alfred Tennyson's Idylls of the King and Other Poems*
Miniature edition
Lincolnshire County Council:
Tennyson Research Centre, Lincoln

This "miniature edition" appeared at about the same time as the second folio volume, and contains twenty-two photographs (most of the material from the folio volumes and two new, untitled pictures).

1. The Dirty Monk
2. Gareth and Lynette
3. Enid from Geraint and Enid
4. ". . . and Enid Sang" from Geraint and Enid
5. Merlin and Vivien "For Merlin overtalk'd and overworn Had yielded, told her all the charm and slept"
6. Elaine, the Lily-maid of Astolat from Lancelot and Elaine
7. Elaine: "So in her tower alone the maiden sat" from Lancelot and Elaine
8. The Parting of Lancelot and Queen Guinevere
9. The little novice and the Queen in "The Holy House at Almesbury"

Cat. 374(15)

Cat. 374(11)

Cat. 373(6)

Cat. 373(4)

10.    King Arthur "The moony vapour rolling round the King who seem'd the Phantom of a giant in it" from Guinevere
11.    "Then spake the King: My house hath been my doom" from The Passing of Arthur
12.    The dead Elaine and the old servitor on the barge from Lancelot and Elaine
13.    "But Arthur spied the letter in her hand" from Lancelot and Elaine
14.    Guinevere "And moved about her palace, proud and pale"
15.    "Then murmur'd Arthur 'Place me in the barge' / So to the barge they came. There those three Queens put forth their hands . . . ' from The Passing of Arthur
16.    The May Queen
17.    The May Queen (dying)
18.    ". . . and a maid of those beside her smote her harp and sang" from The Princess, iv. 38
19.    Maud
20.    The Gardener's Daughter
21.    Mariana
22.    Two Cherubs

## 375
**Julia Margaret Cameron**
Man and Girl [*The Beggar Maid?*]
Photograph 27.9 x 22.8 cms
Lincolnshire County Council:
Tennyson Research Centre, Lincoln

## 376
**Julia Margaret Cameron**
Beggar Girl (Mary Ryan? afterwards Lady Cotton)
*c.*1865
Photograph 23.3 x 28.8 cms
Lincolnshire County Council:
Tennyson Research Centre, Lincoln

## 377
**Julia Margaret Cameron**
Unititled [The May Queen]
Photograph 25.9 x 20.7 cms
Lincolnshire County Council:
Tennyson Research Centre, Lincoln

## 378
**Julia Margaret Cameron**
*"The Rose-bud garden of Girls"*
July 1868
Photograph 35.9 x 32 cms
Lincolnshire County Council:
Tennyson Research Centre, Lincoln

Julia Margaret Cameron refers to *Maud*, I, 902, where the heroine is addressed: 'Queen rose of the rosebud garden of girls'.

# Notes

1. James Joyce, *A Portrait of the Artist as a Young Man* (1916)
2. T.S. Eliot, *In Memoriam* (from *Essays Ancient and Modern*, London, 1936)
3. *Memoir*, II, 430
4. *Martin*, p. 583
5. David Cecil, *Max*, London, 1964; pp. 190-1
6. Andrew Wheatcroft, *The Tennyson Album*, London, 1980; p. 70
7. *Gernsheim*, p. 183
8. Emily Tennyson, *Journal*, ed. with an introduction by James O. Hoge, Charlottesville, 1981; p. 293
9. Lady St. Helier, *Memories of Fifty Years;* pp. 162-3
10. *Martin.* p. 44
11. *Memoir*, I, 12
12. Charles Tennyson and Hope Dyson, *The Tennysons. Background to Genius*, London, 1974; p. 61
13. Francis Hill, *Crackroft Diary;* p. 29
14. *Memoir*, I, 4
15. Markham L. Peacock, Jr, *The Critical Opinions of William Wordsworth*, London, 1950; p. 366
16. *Ricks*, p. 101
17. *Memoir*, I, 12
18. *Memoir*, I, 16
19. *Memoir*, I, 38
20. Jack Kolb (ed.), *The Letters of Arthur Henry Hallam;* p. 172
21. Kolb, p. 391
22. *Martin*, p. 79
23. *Martin*, p. 112
24. *Martin*, p. 88
25. *Martin*, p. 183
26. *Martin*, p. 240-1
27. *Martin*, p. 55
28. Philip Magnus, *Gladstone. A Biography*, London, 1954; p. 6
29. *Memoir*, I, 38
30. *Ricks*, p. 70
31. Daphne Foskett, *John Harden of Brathay Hall, 1772-1847*, Kendal, 1974; p. 45
32. *Martin*, p. 203
33. *Memoir*, II, 462
34. *Memoir*, II, 466
35. *Martin*, p. 200
36. *Martin*, p. 330
37. *Martin*, p. 539
38. *Memoir*, II, 403
39. *Martin*, p. 243
40. Jane Roberts, *Royal Artists*, London, 1987; p. 125
41. *Memoir*, I, 396
42. Sir Charles Tennyson, *Alfred Tennyson*, London, 1949; pp. 289-90
43. Sir Charles Tennyson, *Alfred Tennyson*, London, 1949; p. 289
44. Hallam, Lord Tennyson, *Tennyson and His Friends*, London, 1911; pp. 274-5
45. 'History's Telescope', *The Leader*, 2 September 1855
46. W.M. Rossetti (ed.), *Permanent Photographs after works by Dante Gabriel Rossetti*, 1900; p. 15
47. Norman Page (ed.), *Tennyson. Interviews and Recollections*, London, 1983, p. 128
48. *Gernsheim*, p. 67
49. *Gernsheim*, p. 182
50. *Gernsheim*, p. 181
51. *Gernsheim*, p. 34
52. *Gernsheim*, p. 41
53. *Gernsheim*, p. 46

## Abbreviations:

*Gernsheim*    Helmut Gernsheim, *Julia Margaret Cameron*, New York, 1975.
*Martin*    Robert Bernard Martin, *Tennyson: The Unquiet Heart*, Oxford, 1980.
*Memoir*    Hallam Tennyson, *Alfred Lord Tennyson: A Memoir*, 2 vols., 1897.
*Ricks*    Christopher Ricks, *Tennyson*, Second edition, London, 1989.

# Select Bibliography

William Allingham, *William Allingham's Diary*, London, 1967.

Edward Fitzgerald, *Letters and Literary Remains of Edward Fitzgerald*, ed. W A Wright, 7 vols., 1902-3.

Helmut Gernsheim, *Julia Margaret Cameron*, New York, 1975.

H.R. Haweis, *Poets in the Pulpit*, London, 1880.

Robert Bernard Martin, *Tennyson: The Unquiet Heart*, Oxford, 1980.

Vivian Noakes, *Edward Lear: the Life of a Wanderer*, 1968.

Ruth Pitman, *Edward Lear's Tennyson*, Manchester, 1988

H.D. Rawnsley, *Literary Associations of the English Lakes*, 2 vols., Glasgow, 1901.

H.D. Rawnsley, *Memories of the Tennysons*, Glasgow, 1900.

*Pre-Raphaelite Sculpture - Nature and Imagination in British Sculpture 1848-1914*, ed. Benedict Read and Joanna Barnes, London, 1992.

Christopher Ricks, *Tennyson*, Second edition, London, 1989.

Jane Roberts, *Royal Artists - From Mary Queen of Scots to the Present Day*, London, 1987.

Susan Shatto, *Tennyson's Maud*, 1986.

Charles Tennyson, *Alfred Tennyson*, London, 1949.

Emily Tennyson, *The Letters of Emily, Lady Tennyson*, ed. James O. Hoge, Pennsylvania, 1974.

Emily Tennyson, *Journal*, ed. with an introduction by James O. Hoge, Charlottesville, 1981.

Hallam Tennyson, *Alfred Lord Tennyson: A Memoir*, 2 vols., 1897.

Hallam Tennyson (ed.) *Tennyson and his Friends*, 1911.

Alfred Lord Tennyson, *The Letters of Alfred Lord Tennyson*, 3 vols., ed. Cecil Y Lang and Edgar F. Shannon, Jr, 1982-1991.

Alfred Lord Tennyson, *The Poems of Tennyson*, 3 vols., second edition incorporating the Trinity College Manuscripts, ed. Christopher Ricks, 1987.

*Tennyson in Lincoln: A Catalogue of the Collections in the Research Centre*, compiled by Nancie Campbell, 2 vols., 1971/1973.

*Tennyson: The Critical Heritage*, ed. John D Jump, London, 1967.

*Tennyson: Interviews and Recollections*, ed. Norman Page, London, 1985.

Mike Weaver, *Julia Margaret Cameron 1815-1879*, Southampton, 1984.

Andrew Wheatcroft, *The Tennyson Album - A Biography in Original Photographs*, London, 1980.

# Index